twentysomething

SURVIVING AND
THRIVING IN
THE REAL WORLD

MARGARET FEINBERG

THOMAS NELSON
Since 1798

NASHVILLE DALLAS MEXICO CITY RIO DE JANEIRO BEIJING

Published in Nashville, Tennessee, by Thomas Nelson. Thomas Nelson is a
trademark of Thomas Nelson, Inc.

Thomas Nelson, Inc. books may be purchased in bulk for educational, business,
fund-raising, or sales promotional use. For information, please e-mail
SpecialMarkets@ThomasNelson.com.

Acquisitions and Managing Editor: Lori Jamieson Jones
Editorial Staff: Bethany Bothman, Lauren Weller, Deborah Wiseman, Amanda Corn
Cover Design: Matt Lehman, Nashville, Tennessee
Page Design: Brecca Theele, Book and Graphic Design: Nashville, Tennessee

Scripture quotations, unless otherwise indicated, are taken from The Holy Bible, New International Version (NIV). Copyright © 1973, 1978, 1984, International Bible Society. Used by permission of Zondervan Bible Publishers.

Other Scripture references are from the following sources:

The Living Bible (TLB), copyright © 1971 by Tyndale House Publishers, Wheaton, Ill. Used by permission.

The Message (MSG), copyright © 1993. Used by permission of NavPress Publishing Group.

Library of Congress Cataloging-in-Publication Data

Feinberg, Margaret, 1974–
     Twentysomething: surviving and thriving in the real world / by Margaret
Feinberg.
        p. cm.
     ISBN: 978-0-8499-4444-4
     1. Young adults—Religious life. 2. Young adults—Conduct of life.
I. Title: Twenty something. II. Title.
BV4529.2.F45 2004
248.8'4—dc22   2003020544

Printed in the United States of America
07 08 09 10 11 QW 10 9 8 7 6 5

contents

Acknowledgments vii

Foreword ix

Introduction xiii

One: Rude Awakenings: Grappling with Adult Life   3

Two: The Twentysomething Crisis   29

Three: The Questions That Inhabit the Soul   55
     Where is God in all this?
     Who am I?
     What is my purpose?
     What's really important?

Four: The Questions That Press Us Forward   83
     What the heck am I supposed to do with my life?
     Can I really do it?
     Where do I go from here?

Five: The Questions That Connect Us to Others   109
     Why do I feel alone sometimes?
     Will anyone ever love me?
     Why is no one clapping?
     What is real?

Six: When Hard Times Happen   135

Seven: From Surviving to Thriving   149

Epilogue: Thirtysomething   163

Freebies: Surviving Your First Christmas (or Any
            Major Holiday) Away from Home   169
            Maintaining Friendships from Miles Away   171
            Moving Back in with the Fam   173
            Encouraging Scripture   175
            Low-Fat Snack Options (To Avoid the
                Aforementioned "Secretary Spread")   177
            Nine Tough Job Interview Questions and
                How to Answer Them   179

            Notes   183

            About the Author   187

TO LEIF,
MY LOVE

acknowledgments

Thank you to the dozens of individuals who took the time to respond to a laundry list of questions via phone, e-mail, and late-night discussions. Thank you, particularly, to Norman Wright, John Townsend, Larry Stuenkel, Mike Sares, John Ruhlman, Matt Woodley, Dan Kimball, John Fischer, Brian Habig, Andy Crouch, Christine Beitsch, Ashley and Ted Callahan, Sharon Durling, Bill Haley, Marcia Ford, Chad Pelletier, Rich Hurst, Neil Howe, Dave Terpstra, Jared Mackey, and Lori Smith, whose expertise added greatly to this book.

Thank you to Sheila Frost and Cindy Topping, who helped get this book off the ground late one evening on a storm-tossed boat in south Florida. Thank you for living these twentysomething years alongside me. And thank you to all my beloved friends and family members who read over the manuscript and provided feedback.

My editor, Lori Jones, went above and beyond for me time and time again. Thank you for all your encouragement, feedback, and friendship.

I have a college degree. Biology. I worked and read and procrastinated and crammed and studied and breathed science for four years of my life to get that little piece of paper that says, "Yes, Bebo is a Biologist." Then, somewhere between graduation and the medical school plans that drove it all for four years, I went and got myself a respectable job—I became a musician. I *love* my career. It is my passion and very seldom does it feel like work (there is a reason that it's called "playing" music). So for the last eight years of my life I have laughed and sung and traveled my way around this country and through a career that has been nothing short of a dream come true.

So why is it that I still have found myself at times profoundly lonely and sad and wondering how in the world I ever ended up here? How is it possible to truly love my work, to feel *called* to it even, and still somehow feel so unfulfilled? I have often thought myself spoiled or ungrateful or even shallow but have come to realize through post-concert conversations with so many of my peers around this country that I am not at all alone in this burden. Most all of us have been there. Regardless of our history or our careers or our marital status, we all feel this way at some time or another. How can it be that with all of our planning and preparation, our figuring and formulas, and the latest in intellectual and technological advances that life still manages to fake us all out with such apparent ease and regularity?

The truth is pretty simple. There is no right plan. There is no right way. There is no periodical table for the fundamental elements of *real* life. Here's the secret: *We're all just making this stuff up as we go.* Every single one of us. Even the guy who always gets the job, always fits the bill, and somehow manages to look good doing it. Even the girl who has three beautiful children with one beautiful husband and still lands on the cover of fashion magazines flaunting her great figure. We're all in the same boat.

If we were really honest, we'd *all* admit that regardless of how good life is, regardless of who we live it with or without, and regardless of what we believe or how "well" we believe it, there's still that mysterious *something* that pulls at our souls in an ache for something more. And it doesn't discriminate. Every soul is created with that God-shaped vacuum inside. It's common ground, really. For believers and unbelievers alike. Because we all know, whether we admit it or not, that regardless of how successful our careers may be, or how beautiful and full the relationships in our lives may be, there's something else we long for. Something even more beautiful. Something even more full. I thank God for that part of us. I thank God for the weight of it. I thank God because it's that mysterious something that reminds us that our fullness is never complete until the day we see God face to face.

I just turned thirty. And it has taken every last day of these thirty years for God to make clear to me what Margaret Feinberg has managed to condense into these pages. Margaret speaks to the practical mind and the spiritual heart of what I believe to be the single most transitional figure in modern life—the twentysomething. We are not defined by our careers or our relationships or even our life's passions. God's ultimate and immediate will for our lives as believers becomes simply this: That we would pursue Him *every single day* of our lives. That is what defines us. That is what fulfills us. And the pursuit of that God ultimately is the pursuit of this book.

—BEBO NORMAN

→ There Are Lots of Us: The U.S. Census Bureau estimates there are more than 39 million twentysomethings in the United States.

→ Modest? I Think Not: According to a study by Niagra Spray Starch, 48 percent of 18- to 34-year-olds iron while naked or wearing only their underwear.

I recently read about three women in north Florida who experienced the same symptoms of fever, chills, and vomiting followed by muscular collapse, paralysis, and finally death—all over a five-day period. The women were unrelated. Autopsy reports revealed their common fate: Each had a high toxicity level in her blood. An investigation determined that the women all had eaten at the same Italian restaurant. The health department immediately shut down the restaurant and began a thorough investigation.

Within a few days, a waitress at the restaurant was rushed to a hospital with similar symptoms. She had been on vacation and simply stopped by to pick up her check. She hadn't eaten anything, but she had used the rest room. This clue tipped off one of the toxicologists, who promptly drove to the restaurant, lifted the toilet seat, and noticed a small spider. As suspected, it was a Two-Striped Telamonia, known for its toxic venom. This particular spider prefers dark, damp areas, and the toilet rim had provided a perfect hideaway for the arachnid.

Several days later, a north Florida man who had just returned from a business trip to Indonesia appeared in a hospital emergency room with similar symptoms. Fearing an outbreak, the Civil Aeronautics Board (CAB) inspected the planes and discovered nests not just on one of the planes but on four planes.

It is now believed that these spiders can be anywhere in the country, so if you must use a public rest room, be sure to first lift the seat to look for spiders. This may save your life! PLEASE pass this story on to everyone you care about!

Wait! Actually, please *don't* pass this on to your beloved friends and family. This is a classic urban legend, the kind that contains enough details and believable facts to make you peek under toilet seats in public rest rooms when no one is looking. Despite some of the more ridiculous urban legends—the McPus Sandwich (a fast-food horror story), Bill Gates Shares His Fortune, and Crocodile Eats Golfer (okay, this one may be true)—these myths, passed on through e-mails, are to me humorous refreshers among the onslaught of junk mail I receive each day. They are a lot more interesting than the mounds of spam pitching things like the lowest mortgage rates ever; an at-home business guaranteeing $100,000 a month (could this possibly be legal?); a special pill that promises to enlarge certain anatomy; and a diet miracle drug guaranteed to remove all excess fat in less than thirty days. I'd prefer a little spider paranoia brought on by an urban myth to another slice of spam any day.

It is said that the phrase "urban legend" entered pop culture in the early 1980s with the publication of *The Vanishing Hitchhiker* by Jan Harold Brunvand. It's been defined as "a story, which may have started with a grain of truth, that has been embroidered and retold until it has passed into the realm of myth." As *The Free On-Line Dictionary of Computing* observes, "It is an interesting phenomenon that these stories get spread so far, so fast and so often. Urban legends never die, they just end up on the Internet."[1]

The idea of urban legends and myths has made me reflect on the various ideas that have permeated my own thought life. I have been subject to scads of them—little beliefs such as "There is a soul mate for everyone," and "Credit card debt won't take that long to pay off." While believable, I have learned they just are not for everyone. For someone, somewhere, they may be true, but that person is probably on their fourth marriage and has won the lottery twice in a row.

But the biggest myth I fell for was that launching into the real world is no big deal. That myth began to unravel on graduation day, after the diplomas had been handed out, the caps thrown, and the chairs stacked. I was enjoying the warm embraces of family and friends when I heard my name called over the loudspeaker. I was being asked to come to the front of the podium. Puzzled, I made my way through the crowd. Had there been a mistake—an overlooked award or a misspelling on the diploma? The message was brief: "Call your aunt Teddy in California. It's urgent." A chill went down my spine; I suspected she wasn't calling to offer congratulations.

The next few hours were a blur. Between hugs and handshakes, we managed to find a pay phone. My father made the call, and in a few moments we knew: My grandmother had passed away.

Graduation day—the day I had been anticipating for four years—was overshadowed by a cloud of loss. Instead of joyful celebration, I was facing the cruel, sudden loss of a close family member. None of my loved ones had passed away up until that day. I didn't know how to react, how to respond, or what to do. It all seemed so surreal. This should have been one of the happiest days of my life—graduating with honors from a well-respected private university—but it was interrupted by something far more important: the death of a loved one. A few short hours later, my father and I were in a car driving from North Carolina to Michigan for her funeral.

It was my first lesson of the real world: People die. It seems obvious now, as eventually do most of the lessons or truths people tell you when you are growing up. Everyone seems to understand these lessons and truths, unless, of course, they are happening to you. Unless it's *your* grandmother. Unless it's *your* empty bank account. Unless it's *your* boss saying, "*You're* fired." Unless *you* are the one being thrown out into the real world.

The truth is that entering the real world *is* a big deal. Don't let anyone tell you otherwise. A myriad of practical issues assault the newly independent, including finding a job, managing debt, possibly moving to a new city, making new friends, finding a church, and dealing with roommates. As Janelle Erlichman writes, "This is the life that includes alarm clocks and bosses and bills. Lots and lots of bills."[2] Then, right when you think you've got it all together—after you've conquered paying your rent on time and have something to list under "work experience" on your résumé—entirely new sets of questions rear their ugly heads: *Is this really what I want to do with my life? Am I going to live like this for the rest of my life? What's really important? Am I always going to be alone?*

If you've wrestled with these types of questions, you are not alone. I have interviewed dozens of twentysomethings from all over the United States, and most are dealing with the same bumpy segue into the real world. Their stories are as diverse as their life choices. Some went straight into the work force from high school, others joined the Peace Corps, while others pursued a degree or personal dream. The twentysomethings I've spoken with have candidly discussed their transitions, trials, and triumphs. One of the most interesting things I've discovered is that while the scenarios of all our lives as twentysomethings differ in some regard—location, job title, support network—the core human experience is the same. We share a common bond in the basic challenges we face: struggling during the first year completely on our own, getting out of or staying out of debt, trying to maintain consistent relationships, and all the while trying to get the most out of life.

If you're in your twenties, and you know you don't have all the answers, this book is for you. It's a reminder that in whatever you're facing, you're not alone. Tens of thousands of twentysomethings are facing doubts and fears alongside you, and in the midst of so much change and so many challenges, a wonderful transformation is taking place in each of us. Our twenties really can be some of the best years of our lives, no matter what our landlord, boss, parents, or anyone else says.

I encourage you to sit back and enjoy the ride—not just through the following pages, but also in the years to come.

—MARGARET FEINBERG

P.S. If you're ever in a public rest room and notice a small red spider under your toilet lid, consider using a different stall.

ARE YOU TWENTYSOMETHING?

You know you're in your twenties when

- You have to choose between dinner and a movie or Top Ramen for a week.
- The car in your dreams and the car in your parking slot are completely different.
- Any food that doesn't come in a cardboard box or plastic bag is considered home cooking.
- You put tags from Pier One on the furniture you got from the Salvation Army.

You know you're in the real world when

- You can relate to a "Dilbert" comic strip.
- June is here, and there is no summer vacation in sight.
- You're up to your already receding hairline in debt.
- You're the lowest-paid person in your profession, and you have the pay stubs to prove it.

You know you're in an entry-level job when

- You have a personal access code for every copier in the office.
- You refill your stapler twice a day.
- People don't remember your name, but they remember to harass you for not remembering theirs.
- You ask to go out and pick up everyone's lunch order just to get out of the office.

You know you're on your own when

○ The idea of moving back into your parents' basement sounds cooler all the time.

○ You're collecting rolls of quarters for laundry instead of video games.

○ You're collecting all your other change to pay for gas. (I'd like $2.12 in unleaded, please.)

○ Your mom says she has done the last load of your laundry forever (and she means it this time).

rude awakenings:
grappling with adult life

I don't know what I was thinking. Really, I don't. I thought all those people who got up, got dressed, and drove to work every day really liked what they did. I thought that if nine to five was good enough for them, then it would be good enough for me. I thought my boss would be like my high-school teachers who winked when I missed a day of class. I thought I would make enough money to pay all my bills no matter how much I spent. I thought a lot of things . . . that just weren't true.

Shortly after graduation and my grandmother's funeral, I headed for my first real job. Well, sort of. It was actually a summer internship with a Florida-based publication. The first few days were exciting. I met tons of new people and familiarized myself with the building's layout, especially the small employee kitchen and refrigerator. I immediately made friends with my boss and the coworkers located closest to me. I even had my own cubicle. It was so exciting and new!

I began by organizing my desk and office supplies. Within the first few days, I bought little knickknacks and began decorating my cubicle with photos and conversation starters. I recorded my first greeting on the company's voice-mail system. The process took somewhere between two and three dozen times as I got the "Hello, you've reached the voice mail of . . ." just right. I found a bagel restaurant nearby where I could grab a cup of coffee on my way to work and swing by for a quick lunch in the afternoon. I stocked up on healthy snacks like carrot sticks and granola bars for the afternoon lull in energy. I even had a water bottle. I was ambitious and had everyone (or at least myself) convinced I could do a great job. It was a glorious experience, at least for the first week.

Halfway through the second week, it occurred to me that this wasn't just for fun. Going to work wasn't like spending two weeks at summer camp or a few months abroad, where you could come home afterward. No, the workplace was for keeps, and I would have to keep on working for the rest of my life.

The rest of my life.

Those daunting words hung over my head, and my perception of my work environment suddenly changed. Finding a new Scripto pen in the supply station or connecting with a coworker next to the water cooler lost its wonder. I began to notice my pleasant drive to work in the morning was actually a thirty-five-minute, bumper-to-bumper commute. My cubicle was small. My work was endless. And as nice as all my fellow employees were, their main purpose each day was to get work done, not socialize.

I couldn't believe no one had told me that work was really another four-letter word for *jail.* You have to do your time, eight hours a day, five days a week, fifty weeks a year, with only two weeks off for good behavior. I was deeply jealous of all my college friends who had opted for graduate school. They would be in five-figure (if not six-figure) debt when they got out, but at least they managed to postpone the inevitable prison sentence for a few more years.

I thought my situation was unique until I began asking around and discovered almost everyone had been caught off guard in one way or another. Just to make sure it wasn't just me or a few other coworkers, I called some other recent graduates. At first, they put up the usual front. Everything was going great; they loved their new jobs; they couldn't imagine doing anything else. However, when I pressed a little deeper, they admitted they were struggling, too. The office environment wasn't nearly as fun as college life.

We were all missing our midnight trips to the minimarket for Pop-Tarts, canned cheese, and Wheat Thins. I called a few friends who had accepted positions as youth pastors and worship leaders. They were going through the eye-opening experience of full-time ministry. One friend told me he liked working for the church— except for all the people.

I called a friend who was in the military. After whining about boot camp for forty minutes, he let me know the horrifying truth: The government was not going to let him out of his four-year commitment. He had signed up, and they were going to keep him.

Finally, I called the few friends who had chosen to throw caution to the wind and head to Colorado and Utah to lead wilderness adventure trips, teach skiing, and guide whitewater rafting expeditions. All of them were having the time of their lives. They may have been a month or two behind on those student loan payments, but they were convinced it was well worth the cost (and interest penalties). Jealous and slightly intrigued, I called back a few months later. They admitted that this fun-filled, worry-free lifestyle couldn't last forever—not if they ever wanted to break out of the living-on-Cup-a-Soup-and-cans-of-tuna-with-seven-other-roommates lifestyle. I realized that they would be living my life soon enough. I guess I should have warned them.

CAUGHT BY SURPRISE

No one ever told me that the real world is full of surprises. Maybe everyone assumed I already knew. It wasn't until I graduated and faced a life full of limitless possibilities that I realized how pre-planned my life had been up to that point. Some of the planning can be attributed to the local board of education, but most can be attributed to my parents, who thought it best to make sure their child was educated. Looking back, I realize my life was pretty much planned, and I didn't have a lot to say about it.

I don't remember much before the age of five, except for a few preschool classes and beloved baby-sitters. I remember the day I forgot to wear underwear to kindergarten. Fortunately, I was wearing a long dress that day. But I felt as if every other kindergartner knew. I burst out crying, and it took the teacher nearly half an hour of coaxing for me to confess my little secret. I had to call my mom, and she brought me a pair. After that slightly scarring event, my public education was pretty uneventful.

There weren't too many choices or responsibilities; Mom and Dad took care of the vast majority of them. I went from teacher to teacher and grade to grade until graduation. You probably followed the same progression, unless of course you were brilliant and skipped a grade, or you were a real genius and figured out how to stay in the system for an extra year.

You've probably noticed by now that the current education system has a progression that repeats itself. In each of the segments— elementary, junior high, and high school—you enter the school as the runt of the litter and then grow mentally, physically, and socially until you're the big kid. You may be the runt in kindergarten, but you rule the roost by the end of elementary school. Then disaster strikes, and you're the runt all over again when you enter junior high. This is really obvious in high school, when classes of short, vocally high-pitched, pimply-faced kids enter their first year and emerge four years later the size of an NFL lineman with Barry White's voice or with the physique of a New York City fashion model. This same progression of pipsqueak to king of the hill continues into college and then into the real world, when what we thought would be a great job turns out to be just another runt position with a different title.

Unless you count the runt cycle and a few home economics classes, not a lot of training is given to us for living in the real world. It seems like most school systems and parents think college will provide all of that education. After all, you are away from your parents' rules and structure, living on your own for the first time. But you're still in a bubble of sorts, padded by dorm rooms, cafeteria food, and professors who hopefully want to teach you something first and get recognized in their field second. And the schoolwork? Did you really think an anthropology or political science class would help you earn a big paycheck right after graduation? I was a religion major, and it didn't help me much in covering my first rent check.

"It seems like that first year out of school there's a huge reality check," says Ashley, a 26-year-old graduate of the University of Colorado. "No matter where my friends went—whether they were teaching third grade, working with an advertising agency, or in ministry—across the board, everyone was really struggling."

Ashley says one of the biggest things that happen upon graduation is that you're stripped of all the titles you've had. "You used to be able to say, 'I'm a student or I'm a psychology major, or I'm on a sporting team,' but when you graduate, you have to figure out who you are in the bigger scheme of things. Trying to figure out who you are and what to do in a stage of life that doesn't seem to have much guidance is really hard. I think I learned as much that first year out of college as I did in the four years of college."

No wonder the transition into the working world is so bumpy. No wonder there are so many surprises. No wonder we have been struggling to get our lives settled. For the most part, we're ill-prepared for the realities of adult life. My entrance into the real world, and especially into the work force, was a rude awakening. I had worked jobs before—everything from paper-pushing to pushing plates—but these jobs were always for extra cash. I never had to make sure the amount of my paychecks was actually bigger than the amount of my bills, because Mom and Dad were always paying the heating and gas bills, stocking the refrigerator, and filling up the tank whenever I wasn't driving the car. I was smart enough to know these things didn't just magically happen, but I didn't comprehend what it would be like to make them happen myself. Most things managed to catch me off guard, but I've managed to sift through the rather long list and identify the top ten. Who knows? Maybe they'll find a spot on *The Late Show* with David Letterman one day.

1. You Have to Work

I knew that one day I would have to work—everyone has to work. I didn't know that I would have to work every day until I had built up enough of this substance called retirement money to never work again. And all the while I was trying to build up a retirement reservoir, the little demands of life would be eating away at my goal of not having to work.

Thomas, a 26-year-old graduate of the University of Alaska, says the hardest part of transitioning to the real world for him was having to work all the time. "I can't be lazy like I could at home," he says. "Now I have to buy my own shoes, not to mention my wife's and kids'."

Do you remember the days when a note from a parent was enough to excuse you from class? In school, you enjoyed the benefits of a summer vacation: three full months of fun and sun, an easy job, and lots of potential dates. In the real world, my bosses weren't satisfied with a note from Mom or the explanation that I really needed a day to relax. They wanted me at work *every* day, for the *entire* day. After checking with a doctor, I discovered all the illnesses that make it impossible to sit at a desk and work are too embarrassing to submit to an employer.

For a while, the teaching profession, with its promise of summers off, sounded great, but my fear of being trapped in a classroom with two dozen junior high kids made me reconsider. The military, with its retirement plan, sounded interesting, too, until I learned that boot camp isn't optional. The idea of marrying someone for money sounded okay, until I realized if I did that, I probably would never be able to live with myself morally. Somehow I also managed to overcome the temptation to sell everything I owned to a pawnshop, buy a stack of lottery tickets, and pray for the jackpot.

2. Entry-Level Jobs Aren't Always Fun

Before graduating, my biggest challenge was landing a job, but little did I know an even bigger challenge was waiting: the entry-level (a.k.a. runt) position.

Those graduating from school find themselves in the great Catch-22 of the working world—to get a job, you need experience, but to get experience, you need a job. The result is that most graduates find themselves in an entry-level position, on the lowest rung of the working-world ladder. These positions tend to be . . . well, let's just be honest: the bottom of the food chain. To make us feel a little better, bosses trick us with glorified titles. We may be able to fool some people by telling them we're an administrative assistant when we are a secretary, a retail consultant when we are a salesclerk, or an information specialist when we're doing data entry eight hours a day, but we can't fool ourselves.

Listening to all the statistics about the job market these days, I am grateful just to have a job. But how many times can you restock supplies, replace the toner cartridge, and staple, staple, staple without wondering, *Is this all there is? Is this what four years of college gets you? And shouldn't the highlight of my day be bigger than a trip out of the office to the copy shop?*

Gillian, a 24-year-old library cataloger, describes her transition to the real world as "pretty bumpy." After graduation, she was dating someone, and neither of them had a clear idea of the career path they wanted to follow. Gillian says she was happy doing the college thing—classes, hanging out with friends, enjoying a relaxed schedule—but was looking forward to not having to study when the reality of the nine to five of life hit her between the eyes.

"I couldn't fathom how anyone could work eight hours a day," she recalls. "When were you supposed to get anything done? When could you meet for lunch with friends or go running or just sit at a coffee shop and read? I was definitely unprepared for the time commitment a full-time job required. In some ways, I was very immature and unknowing about the real world and didn't want to get into the daily grind."

Entry-level jobs will forever remain humbling. That's how they're designed. They remind you of what you really *don't* want to be doing for the rest of your life and help you decide to work hard, do a good job, and progress to the next job level as quickly as possible. The good news is that despite whatever you're feeling, entry-level jobs really don't last forever, and after a little while your responsibilities and pay will increase, even if you don't get the corner office and a reserved parking space. Entry-level jobs are a much-needed reminder that you are not what you do. Your value and worth reside elsewhere. And, hopefully, the experience reminds you to treat the next person who does your job a little better.

3. Moving Up in the World Takes Lots of Hard Work

They say it over and over again: *You have to pay your dues just like everyone else.* I have listened to this statement for several years now and have finally concluded no one ever tells you how much those dues will cost. No one ever tells you when those dues will finally end. No one ever tells you who is actually getting paid all those dues.

I knew I would have to pay my dues, but I never knew I'd have to pay them for so long. I assumed I'd be given "the big break" documented in so many of VH1's "Behind the Music" and Biography Channel stories. I honestly believed that someday someone would come along and help me see something in myself that I didn't know was there. Doors would fly open, my purpose would be clear, and all my dues would be paid in full.

Instead of being a hopeless romantic, I was a hopeless optimist, or at least partially delusional. It only took a few rounds of "Could you deliver this file to so-and-so?" to wake up and discover that the big break wasn't necessarily around the next corner, and I needed to brace myself for the long haul.

Over the last few years, I've discovered that life isn't about one big break. It's about a series of little breaks, or opportunities, that God entrusts to us. They come at odd times, usually unexpected, and rarely without increased responsibilities. You have to pay your dues. You have to pay a lot of them. And in the end, the difference between those who make it and those who don't is simple: You have to decide to never give up.

4. Life Is Expensive

This may sound a little crazy, but after years of careful study, I am convinced that black holes exist on our planet. And there are at least two main areas where they hover. First, they tend to hang over my car keys, which mysteriously disappear whenever I put them down. Second, they gravitate toward my checking and savings accounts and devour all excess funds. Really. I can testify to this.

There will be an extra $20 or $30 in my account one day, and the next day, it's gone. Scientists may try to point to the empty pizza boxes in my trash can to explain the strange phenomenon, but they're just looking for a loophole.

The truth is that life is expensive. Rent goes up and cars break down. Whether it's eating out, buying gifts, or replacing your workout shoes, most things cost more than you'd think. You can find a bargain here or there—a shirt for half off or a discounted treasure on eBay—but those little things are there just to make you feel better about the big things that are taking all your money, like student loans and revolving credit card debt, both of which can be out of control. In 2000, the average student loan debt for a full-time student from a four-year university was almost $17,000, nearly double what it was a decade ago. Meanwhile, 41 percent of all graduating seniors carried credit card debt of more than $3,000. But even if you can manage those two debt monsters, there are still all the expenses you didn't count on in your monthly budget (assuming you have one), like a semiprofessional wardrobe, a transmission problem with your car, or a minor surgery that results in major bills.[1]

There is also that little word that has a big price tag: *insurance.* I was hoping the insurance company was just kidding when they said I was no longer eligible to be on my parents' insurance policy after turning 23. I knew the insurance company was serious about other issues, but I really thought they'd make an exception just for me. After all, my family had been great clients for years. In all that fine print, somewhere, I expected to find a clause that would allow me to keep my health insurance. I called the company. I cried. I argued. And I lost. I felt like I had been rejected by the mean-spirited chef at the Soup Kitchen on *Seinfeld,* but instead of being told, "No soup for you!" I was being told, "No insurance for you!"

The insurance company isn't the only one that doesn't make exceptions. Just because you are kind, know someone, or have a great smile doesn't mean an exception is going to be made for you. Sure, they may have made one in the past, but that doesn't mean you're always going to find a loophole.

As soon as I learned how expensive life really is, I moved back in with Mom and Dad.

5. You May Have to Move Back Home

For some, this is a joy. For others, this is a nightmare. Many of my high-school friends say they felt like a failure because they never left their hometown or they had to move back. When you have the entire world ahead of you, it can be humbling to choose to return to your hometown, especially when it's a small one.

Even more humbling than moving back home is moving back in with Mom and Dad. You may have to face the stigma that is attached to reinvading the parental nest. You may even have to sleep on the couch for a few weeks while your parents reconvert the home office (which used to be your bedroom) back into a bedroom.

The good news is, this stigma is fading away as more and more twentysomethings move back home for a season or two. Roughly 10 percent of adults ages 25 to 34 are living with their parents, double the percentage living with Mom and Dad fifty years ago. In fact, Jobtrak and Monstertrak both report 60 percent of college seniors expect to return home and live with their parents, and 21 percent expect to live there for more than a year.[2]

People who choose to move back in with their parents are able to slash debt at a much quicker rate and therefore give up less of their income to the interest payment on their loans. Financially, people who move in with their parents are winning, even though they aren't as cool as everyone living in a posh studio apartment (and eating Top Ramen noodles when no one is looking).

I was a little apprehensive about moving home, but I discovered something wonderful. On top of the financial benefits, living at home helped to renew my relationship with my parents. It also helped me learn how to handle adult responsibilities slowly, rather than jumping in with both feet. When something in the house broke, I wasn't calling Dad from a few states away asking for advice. I could watch him fix it and in the process learn how to repair it myself. I learned how to handle responsibilities—whether it was training a new dog or fixing the roof. The great thing was that I could do it all with someone nearby to help if I got into trouble. Overall, I can honestly say that it was a great experience, and I wouldn't trade it for the world.

6. Finding Friends, Church, and Community Isn't Always Easy

When I look in the mirror, I see someone who is adventurous and outgoing. I see someone who doesn't have any problems making friends. I can help you pick out the perfect pair of skis or a snowboard, reel in a big fish, and cook a healthy meal for ten in a moment's notice, never forgetting to discreetly tell you about that broccoli stuck between your teeth before anyone else notices. I am great best-friend material. So why is it that I am having a hard time making friends in a new city? When you put me in a large city with a potential for a million or so new friends, I struggle to connect with anyone, let alone a million people. How am I supposed to develop lifelong friendships when I am struggling to connect with anyone?

In today's highly mobile culture, people are constantly drifting in and out of my life; at the same time, I am drifting in and out of their lives. It is a wonderfully enriching process, except when it happens all at once. In school, I developed friendships that I knew would last a lifetime. Our relationships were built around common experiences and interests. After graduation, though, we each packed up our individual vehicles and headed in different directions. Some went to the police academy. Others went to law school. Some headed to corporations, and others went into the military. Some decided to start their own companies, and others decided to pursue artistic dreams or outdoor adventures.

Most of my friends headed to the Northeast, landing in Washington, D.C., Philadelphia, and New York City, while I chose to follow the snowbirds to central Florida. I had no idea how much I'd miss those late nights eating pizza and pretending to study. I quickly learned that getting a "real" job takes up far more hours in a day than my schoolwork did. And all that working leaves little energy and time for building friendships. When I finally manage to carve out time in my busy schedule to do something, I have to find someone who can carve out the same time and who wants to do the same thing. Solid friendships don't just happen; they take time, sacrifice, and intentional effort, and making friends was a lot more difficult than I thought it would be.

As if finding friends wasn't enough, I also had to find a church I could call home. In a big city, you'd think this would be a cakewalk; after all, the listing of churches in the Yellow Pages takes up a half-dozen pages. But after a few months of visiting congregations, I was still looking for a place that I could call home. I found myself lost in the bigger churches and uncomfortable surrounded by families with children in the smaller congregations. I went to churches that offered a meat market for singles, and others that didn't have anyone between 20 and 40 in the congregation. Some churches offered phenomenal times of worship but shallow Bible teaching; others provided great teaching but stale times of worship. After two months of Wednesday evening, Saturday night, and Sunday morning services, I finally discovered a church in a nearby town that was worth the extra driving to attend. Thinking I had it made, I struggled to build relationships with other twentysomethings who lived so far away. Finding a church where I felt welcome and comfortable was a lot more difficult than I ever anticipated.

I've talked to scads of twentysomethings who also struggle to find a church community they feel comfortable in. Brian, a 24-year-old living in Nashville, Tennessee, said it took him almost three years to find a church he could call home. "I started asking around in college and started going with friends, but didn't like it much," he says. "It was too much marketing to the rich and performance and not enough God. When I go to church, I want to know that there are real Christians there worshiping God. I don't want to feel like it's just a routine. I spent a lot of weekends having my own church at the house or by the lake. The Lord finally led me to an awesome church with a large young adult crowd."

The good news is that most twentysomethings who are persistent, and willing to attend a different denomination than the one they grew up in, find a great church they can call home sooner or later.

7. It's Hard to Find That Special Someone

My four years of college were preceded by well-meaning family and friends who said, "I just know you'll meet *the one* while you're in school."

They were so wrong.

I didn't find *the one;* instead, I found a bunch of other guys, some good ones and some bad ones. And like most in my class, I graduated single.

I headed into my twenties bold and brash and wasn't too concerned about settling down. Then my twenty-seventh birthday appeared, and I realized something strange had happened: I was still single. Now, I might be a little slow on the uptake, but sometime during that next year I realized what a prime opportunity school had been to meet someone. Those well-meaning family members and friends had known something all along. When I wanted to meet someone at college, I attended a function or event. When I wanted to meet someone in the real world, the options were less appealing: a bar or singles event. I'm still not sure which is worse. The kind of guy I wanted to meet wasn't going to frequent either one.

James, a 29-year-old living in Steamboat Springs, Colorado, describes his transition into the real world as a "work in progress." "It has been incredibly difficult learning to be alone," he says. "Working, paying my mortgage and bills, and living life in general are not a problem; not having anyone around to share my thoughts and dreams with is a very daunting task. I struggle with it on a daily basis and constantly wonder if it will ever get any easier."

Finding someone you want to spend the rest of your life with isn't easy. Some people join a dating service, while others log on, trying to find an Internet love connection. Some people find romance through a small group at church, while others meet that special someone at work. For many years, my personal dream has been to meet someone in the produce aisle of the grocery store. I picture him standing among the melons, a big, strong fellow who loves the outdoors and thinks that grilled chicken breast and steamed broccoli are manna from heaven. But that hasn't happened. I listened to what felt like fifty bazillion stories of other people falling in love and marrying before I finally said, "What about me?!" Maybe you've asked that same question, too, along with several others: *When will my day come? Will it ever come? Where is that special someone?* It's easy to grow discouraged by the lack of possibilities—or even the abundance of possibilities, especially if the possibilities are blind dates set up by well-meaning friends. If you're struggling to find *the one,* you're not alone.

8. Even in Your Twenties, the Body Begins to Show a Few Faint Signs of Aging (Gasp!)

I once asked my mom if she felt any different as she grew older. While she still remains active—diving, skiing, and hiking—she says her recovery time has changed. She gets more tired and stays sore a little longer.

Fortunately, I am still in my twenties and can do the same physical activities as before without much concern about payback time the next day. One glaring exception to this rule is sleep. Like most students, I used to be able to pull all-nighters. Now I can't stay up all night even if I try. Somewhere between 3 a.m. and 5 a.m., my head starts to pound, my vision begins to blur, and my body aches. I literally hurt from the lack of sleep. I may try to catch up by sleeping in that morning and going to bed early the following night, but sleep deprivation takes a heavy toll.

The recovery time just isn't the same, and even if I try to deny it, it seems as if the glory days are over. My friend Peter calls it the Party Poopers Club. A group of twentysomethings will get together on a weeknight, and by 9:30 p.m., everyone is heading home to get some sleep so they can work the next day. Some people call it being a responsible adult, but I like Peter's title better.

The battle of the bulge also becomes a little tougher sometime during the twenties. The good news is that the Freshman Fifteen—those dozen-plus pounds you gain during school—aren't a problem once you graduate. The bad news is, they aren't a concern because you're too busy worrying about the Secretary Spread from a desk job or the I-don't-have-time-to-cook-so-I'll-just-eat-at-_____(insert the name of your favorite restaurant here) poundage.

Wade, a 29-year-old graduate student of Loyola Marymount University in Los Angeles, California, estimates that he has gained forty pounds since college. "I look more and more like my dad every day," he says. "And I'm losing my hair. I'm cutting it shorter, but overall, I'm letting nature run its course. No Rogaine for me! I try to work out, but it's very hard considering I now work full-time and am finishing grad school at night."

You can try to fight it. You can join Gold's Gym. You can join the buyer's discount program at GNC. You can lift weights, run, walk, bike, or get involved in any other sport. And it will make a difference. John, a 26-year-old intern with Young Life, said he is the strongest he's ever been. "My body fat percentage is average to below average, and this is coming from a former fat kid," he said. "Sure, there are a few signs of aging like a receding hairline—that's why I shave my head—a few more aches and pains, and I don't recover from lack of sleep like I used to, but I don't have any complaints. I'm happy."

Your body doesn't stop changing after adolescence; the changes have just begun. Your metabolism begins to slow down and your weight starts to creep up. I've also already noticed that a few strands of my hair have made their own independent decisions to turn gray. It's all part of the aging process, and while it's important to take care of your body, the sooner you come to terms with these inevitable changes, the healthier you'll be—physically and emotionally.

9. You Don't Have to Leave the Country to Experience Culture Shock

I grew up in Steamboat Springs, Colorado. It's a mountain town, complete with a ski area, ice rink, and rodeo grounds. While I have never had the desire to climb Mount Everest, I thoroughly enjoy the outdoors. I love hiking, river rafting, horseback riding, skiing, and car camping. I enjoy picking spring flowers and crunching along on fall leaves. When I'm outside, I feel alive.

While other women are shopping at Ann Taylor and Dillard's, I'm at Eddie Bauer scouring the off-season clearance racks and stocking up on sweaters, turtlenecks, fleeces, and wool socks. If you've spent any time in the outdoors, you know functionality is more important than appearance. Who cares if it's cute if it doesn't keep you warm? As a result, my clothes are usually a size too big but just right for easy layering, and my backpack is usually stuffed with at least ten pounds of just-in-case supplies.

My move to North Carolina for college wasn't too much of a stretch as far as attire was concerned. There were plenty of outdoor enthusiasts and grunge heads there, so I blended in; but when I arrived in Orlando, I didn't exactly fit in. Everyone seemed to be driving two-wheel-drive sporty cars, while I was huffing around in my Subaru (affectionately dubbed the "grocery-getter" by some friends because it was a station wagon). I knew better than to bring my sweaters and jackets to Florida, but I didn't realize just how different the clothes in my closet looked until I noticed the form fitting fashions everyone else was wearing. Even though the seasons barely changed, other women's wardrobes did—regularly. Having new and trendy clothes mattered, and I didn't have anything reeking of modern fashion, unless a few timeless pieces like white T-shirts and jeans qualify as haute couture.

In Colorado, people don't ask what you do or what you drive as long as they know what kind of board, or skis, you have under your feet. Catching the handful of primo powder days on the mountain is more important than a high-paying job that requires you to work all the time. But in cities like Orlando, your car and the title on your business card *do* matter. Growing up in a city of ten thousand and then trying to survive in a city of 1.5 million was a little overwhelming. Scratch that. *A lot* overwhelming. The urban splendor caught me off guard. Traffic. Pollution. People everywhere. When I walked down the sidewalk, I couldn't tell who might want to mug me. I would get lost regularly and end up in a sketchy area of town and not realize it until someone the next day gave me the "You went *where???*" speech. I tried to get my coworkers to do something cool like go tubing down a river or hiking in a preserve, and they looked at me blankly, smiled, and informed me they were going to a concert or show on the weekend. I definitely discovered that I didn't need to go abroad to experience culture shock. A move from the West to the East Coast was enough for me.

For you it might be just the reverse: A move from a big city to a small one may cause the shock. For others, moving from one region of the country to another causes culture shock. As much as I say that I'm not, I really am a creature of habit. I don't roll with the punches as I think I should. But I've decided that whether I'm in the great outdoors or the concrete jungle, I can try to make the best of it.

10. I Know Less Than I Thought I Did (and I Didn't Know Much)

Youthful exuberance convinces every teenager they know more—a lot more—than they actually do. I was no exception. I knew a lot, at least until I was smart enough to figure out I didn't know anything. Somewhere between my first English exam and the end of my freshman semester, I discovered I had a lot of learning to do. And all that learning wasn't going to end anytime soon. During school, I studied the great philosophers, mathematicians, theologians, astronomers, and thinkers of history, but knew very little about surviving in the real world. I could quote facts about American history, but actually handling conflict between two friends was a lot more difficult.

My 28-year-old friend Cindy developed a reference term for our knowledge of life. She calls it "three-by-five cards." Whenever I call her for advice on a situation, she'll offer wisdom on how to respond or react, unless it is a situation she has never heard before. Then her voice will soften, and she'll say, "Marg, I don't have a *three-by-five card* on that one. I don't know what to tell you."

Three-by-five cards record experiences and knowledge, but in the course of everyday life, you'll encounter new people and situations that throw you for a loop. No matter how much you know, or think you know, another situation is waiting to trip you up. Your stack of three-by-five cards is pretty thick when you're young, and you think you have all the answers, but all you've really got is a lot of blank cards.

The truth is that each day I'm learning more, but the greatest thing I'm discovering is that I still have a lot more to learn.

THE REAL WORLD

All the realities that caught me by surprise can be summed up in one statement: The real world isn't anything like *The Real World* on MTV.

Chadwick Pelletier, who starred in *Road Rules: Australia* and later married Holly Brentson, who starred in *Road Rules: South Africa,* says, "*Real World,* the television show, is everything but real. Put it this way . . . the show caters to a preteen to mid-twentysomething demographic, who would be bored out of their minds if they knew what really happened during the show. And that's the truth."

Although I believe Chad's insider information that all is not as it seems on these shows, I have a confession to make: I have applied to be on more reality television shows than I care to admit. To support my little addiction, I've conned multiple friends into making short and corny videos, filled out twelve-plus-page application forms with thoughtful and sometimes provocative answers, and even overnighted the information to studios in order to meet their deadlines.

My interest in reality television started in my teens with MTV's homegrown *The Real World* and *Road Rules*. At 29, I am too old to apply to either one (the cutoff age was 26 the last time I checked), but thanks to the networks hopping on board with their own, I have an ever-growing list of new shows to which I can apply. Not only do I apply to be on reality television shows, I also watch them. I am guilty of hosting *Survivor* parties, watching *Big Brother,* staring in disbelief and wonder at ABC's *Extreme Makeover,* and watching almost the entire season of *The Bachelor.* And, yes, when no one is looking, I even watch *Fear Factor.* I often wonder: Why watch scripted characters—other than those on *Friends,* of course—when you can watch real people have real meltdowns on national television?

Much has been written about our society's fascination with reality TV, but a friend of mine summed up the trend in a simple observation: "It's human chess." We love the opportunity to watch people interact outside their natural environment and in the process learn something about ourselves. It's fun to watch a season of other people's blunders—a lot more enjoyable than going through a season like that ourselves.

There are days, however, when I wish the real world really was like *The Real World.* Even if it's only make-believe, I wish someone would sponsor my life for a few months. A posh crib in a cool city, new friends, and a big project to accomplish all sound pretty great. If the only things I had to worry about every day were getting along with a few obnoxious roommates and trying not to make a you-know-what out of myself on national television, life wouldn't be so bad.

But I don't live in *The Real World.* I live in the real world without the deluxe accommodations or cameras making me famous. I can't be just an audience member watching other people make mistakes; I am a participant who is learning most of life's lessons the hard way. When the rent is due, I have to pay it. When I want food to eat, I have to cook it. When the sponge by the kitchen sink smells sour, I have to bleach it. It's real life. Every day. And I'm learning.

→ An Appetite on the Go: Americans ages 24 to 35 average only five home-cooked meals a week. Many want their home to be close to a restaurant. (Boyce Thompson, "X Marks the Spot," *Builder,* February 2001, 21.)

→ Looking Good: For those under 25, the average income before taxes is $19,744. Of that, it's estimated $1,420, or 7.2 percent, of the income is spent on apparel. ("The WWD List: The Age of Affluence," *WWD,* August 29, 2002, 10.)

→ Moving On: According to the Bureau of Labor Statistics, the median stay at jobs by workers in their early twenties has been halved—from 2.2 years in 1983 to 1.1 years today. ("Insurance Gets Hip," *American Demographics,* January 1, 2002, 48.)

→ Moving Around: Forty-five percent of Americans ages 24 to 35 expect to move within the next two years. (Boyce Thompson, "X Marks the Spot," *Builder,* February 2001, 21.)

MARK ALL THAT APPLY TO YOUR PRESENT STATE OF MIND

○ I should be further along in life than I am now.

○ I don't want to grow up.

○ I feel overwhelmed by the number of options available.

○ I never got a road map to life.

○ I frequently get stressed out.

○ I feel pressured to succeed.

○ I second-guess my career and life decisions, especially when I compare myself to friends.

○ I feel depressed by the lack of options.

○ I am still trying to figure out who I am.

○ Some days I quietly wonder, *Is this all there is?*

○ I feel a significant amount of instability in my life.

○ I feel like no one really understands.

If the number of statements you marked total

7–12: You're in the quarterlife crisis! But be encouraged, you're not alone.

4–6: You're definitely experiencing aspects of the quarterlife crisis.

0–3: You have it pretty much together and either have not hit the quarterlife crisis or are on your way out. You can be a source of encouragement and strength to others who are going through it.

the twentysomething crisis

Sometime in my midtwenties I woke up and began asking a question that few people, especially Christians, dare to ask aloud: "Is this all there is?" I loved my work, I loved my friends, and I loved God, but I couldn't help wondering if there was something more. This longing for more, in a society that seemed to offer so much, couldn't be quenched. My questions grew into discontentment and finally discouragement. Some days, and this is hard for anyone—especially someone in the church—to admit, I felt depressed.

I received the same book for my graduation from both high school and college—*Oh, the Places You'll Go!* by that rhyme-on-time creative genius, Dr. Seuss. Maybe you received a copy, too. The book is a popular gift for graduations because it's an inspirational launching pad into the next stage of life, promising success, achievement, and the fulfillment of childhood dreams.

Written in a rhyme as familiar as *Green Eggs and Ham,* Dr. Seuss encourages us that with "brains in your head" and "feet in your shoes" even you can "steer yourself any direction you choose." He sends readers flying and leaping with promises: "You'll be on your way up! You'll be seeing great sights! You'll join the high fliers who soar to great heights!"[1]

Every so often I'll pick up one of my copies of *Oh, the Places You'll Go!* and wonder why Dr. Seuss didn't do a better job of warning me. Sure, he mentioned that there would be slumps and waiting places, but he didn't tell me how long those slumps or seasons of waiting would last. Why? Probably because Dr. Seuss didn't want to burst my bubble. He didn't want to remind me that there would be so many things standing between a diploma and all those places I was supposed to go. Dr. Seuss didn't tell me about all the job applications, résumés, rejection letters, endless bills, romantic breakups, and grumpy roommates, not because he didn't know about them, but because he wanted to write an encouraging book. Besides, how many words really rhyme with "job application" and "grumpy roommate"? Even Dr. Seuss had his limits.

Though Dr. Seuss never wrote specifically about the quarterlife crisis,* that doesn't mean it's not real. Just ask any twentysomething who is struggling with the harsh realities of adulthood. In case you've never really heard about the quarterlife crisis, it is a younger brother to the midlife crisis that often hits full-fledged adults in their forties. Typically, middle-aged men respond by buying a red convertible sports car, cheating on their spouse after twenty-plus years of marriage (or trading her in for a trophy wife), refurbishing

---

* Alexandra Robbins and Abby Wilner, *Quarterlife Crisis* (Los Angeles: J.P. Tarcher, 2001.)

their wardrobe with the latest styles, getting a trendy haircut (or worse, trying to grow a goatee), or becoming depressed. Women who go through a midlife crisis are often beginning the emotional roller coaster of menopause, tend to either gain or lose twenty pounds, date a younger guy to feel better about themselves, or pay visits to a plastic surgeon.

The quarterlife crisis doesn't usually manifest itself in such colorful terms, but it does include an identity crisis of sorts, coupled with a longing to postpone adult responsibilities (or at least run away from them for a while) and a possible leap into an entirely new profession, career, business, location, or relationship.

The term was made famous by Alexandra Robbins and Abby Wilner in their book *Quarterlife Crisis,* and they agree that it is similar to a midlife crisis, except that it occurs twenty years earlier. The authors assess that the quarterlife crisis is a response to "overwhelming instability, constant change, too many choices, and a panicked sense of helplessness."[2]

It's what happens when those of us who have experienced nearly two decades in a sheltered school setting are released into a world where there is no definitive or obvious way to get from point A (graduation) to point B (living successfully on our own). The endless list of choices and possibilities invigorates some but proves overwhelming to others. The quarterlife crisis is everything that surfaces when you begin asking the question, *What the heck am I doing with my life?* And begin quietly wondering, *Who am I? What is my purpose?* and *Where is God in all this?*

The quarterlife crisis happens to twentysomethings who find themselves overrun in a fast-paced world, feeling the pressure to succeed in an environment that is filled with uncertainty. For some, the environment creates a high level of expectation and hope, but for others, there are underlying fears including the fear of failure, the fear of rejection, or the fear of not fitting in.

The transition into the real world puts twentysomethings into a posture of having to play catch-up. Think about it. After a life of going to school, you are out in the real world and expected to know how to do everything when, in fact, you really don't know how to do anything. Instead of feeling like a twenty "something," some days you feel like a twenty "nothing." Sure, you can tie your shoes, recite the ABCs, and count to eighty-seven before becoming grossly bored. But do you know who is the best pick for managing your retirement account, how to handle an emotionally unstable boss, or where the best place is in town for pizza? (Okay, at least you know one out of three!) No matter what Robert Fulghum may say, everything you need to know, you didn't learn in kindergarten.

Many experience a type of emotional roller coaster from the challenges of being a twentysomething. "The twenties are such a turbulent time in your life," says Rebekah, a 28-year-old living near Kansas City, Kansas. "At different times throughout your midtwenties, you feel like you're on this enormous roller coaster that is going so high up and so far down and at any second, anything could happen. At times, the sky really does feel like the limit and miracles are within your reach, and on the flip side you're barely hanging on."

The quarterlife crisis has its naysayers just as the midlife crisis does. Reportedly, when Robbins and Wilner (authors of *Quarterlife Crisis*) appeared on the *Today* show and discussed the topic, Katie Couric expressed skepticism. When they appeared on *Oprah,* the daytime diva offered empathy. Others believe the quarterlife crisis is just an ordinary stage of early adulthood.

Stacey Humes-Schulz wrote in an editorial in the *Daily Pennsylvanian,* "The quarterlife crisis is not the result of pure career anxiety. It is the product of the luxury of a simple life at elite private schools. . . . The real world that some of us have been sheltered from until now is filled with tough decisions. But to be blunt, suck it up."[3]

WRESTLING WITH THE QUARTERLIFE CRISIS

While not everyone experiences a quarterlife crisis, many will attest that the internal struggle that takes place during your twenties is very real. The quarterlife crisis can be particularly disheartening for twentysomething Christians who find themselves in a church culture where the institution really doesn't know what to do with them. Many churches are quick to remind believers that God loves them and has a wonderful plan for their lives but are slow to admit that part of the plan includes growing pains, adversity, and failure.

At 23, Dexter, a graduate of the Brownsville Revival School of Ministry in Pensacola, Florida, followed in the footsteps of his father and entered the ministry. He works with a small congregation in the Northeast. I've known him for several years, and he carries a contagious passion for God. However, he, too, hit a recent crisis point:

"God loves me, right? Why, then, does my heart feel betrayed? My mom is in the hospital suffering from pneumonia, and I'm sick with the flu. My dad is on the verge of a nervous breakdown, and I don't think I've ever been so stressed in my life. I make only $100 a week and have mounting bills. No need to e-mail me back right when you get this . . . just do some praying for me . . . I can't."

A few weeks later, Dexter sent me a note letting me know that things were getting better. His mom had been released from the hospital, and his dad had gone on a much-needed retreat. God had proved Himself faithful through the trials. Reflecting on the experience and the past year or so of his life, Dexter says he has been experiencing the quarterlife crisis without knowing what to call it.

"The experience was stressful and full of destructive possibilities," Dexter explains. "Without great Christian friends around me, surrounding me with prayer, I would not have made it. The experience included depression, asking doubtful questions about my existence and my calling in life: a dark night of the soul, where it seemed as though my Creator had forgotten me in the lab of life somewhere, and I wasn't getting my daily provisions. Along with it were lots of stress and tears—sometimes for no reason—and yet I feel that I wasn't in the wrong or sinning and being punished; it was just happening, and no one asked me if I wanted it."

The doubts and questions Dexter expressed are characteristic of the quarterlife crisis. Not only was Dexter wrestling with the practical issues of work, finances, and family, but he was also struggling to figure out how God fit into the framework of faith. Sometimes finding God when you are at a crisis point is like trying to locate Waldo in one of those picture books. You just know the guy wearing the red-and-white-striped sweater is on the page somewhere, but as hard as you look for the distinct colors, his glasses, or his beady eyes, you just can't find him. In the same way, God is in every situation—including a quarterlife crisis—but sometimes He's hard to find in the midst of all that's going on.

Take this rather personal excerpt from my journal as a snapshot of my quarterlife crisis:

Dear God,

I'm struggling. You know it. I've been struggling for a while. In the face of no work, unable to pay the electric bill or January quarterly tax payment, I finally broke. Tired of walking to the mailbox day after day for over sixty days and still not finding the money owed to me, I collapsed. In exhaustion. In frustration. In utter brokenness. I was ready to quit. I couldn't bear any more rejection.

That season has passed. Seemingly overnight a flood of work has arrived. The bills will be paid. The debt will be erased. Thank You, God! Everything has changed, but my heart is still bruised. I wonder how long I can bear the burden of not knowing when the next paycheck will come and if I'll be paid at all. I wonder if I'll ever be able to live alone or afford a home or have any sort of retirement or if the fight to make enough money to survive will ever end.

I love You, Lord, but shopping at garage sales and Goodwill for clothes gets old. Living with roommates, having to put things on the credit card just to survive till the next check comes when turning 30 is around the corner is disheartening. The constant battle to find work is exhausting. And I wonder how much longer I can keep up the pace. Lord, I'm tired. I look at my friends—who are interning at the Mayo Clinic, finding placement in law firms, driving fine automobiles, and buying homes—and it's hard. They've chosen lucrative professions. I've chosen the one that You placed in my heart. I'm

not in Africa. I'm not even in ministry. But sometimes I still
feel like I'm paying a cost for following You—for following
Your will for my life. I believe this is Your will for my life. If I
didn't, I'd climb the tallest corporate ladder I could find. But
this thing—this desire to write and the joy I find in it—seems
inescapable. It's dark right now, Lord. I don't know when the
storm will break.

That was just one of my quarterlife crisis moments, caused by financial strain. A lack of money causes many twentysomethings to question their lives. While the quarterlife crisis is one watershed moment for some, for others, like myself, it comes in waves and steadily breaks over the soul.

Parents can play a big role in the quarterlife crisis. Some parents pay or choose to pay for college tuition, while others cannot pay or choose not to pay. Some parents choose to financially support their children right on into their thirties, while other parents sever all financial support as soon as the child leaves the house. Most parents fall somewhere in between.

Matt, a 27-year-old graduate of the University of Alabama, was going through a quarterlife crisis moment. He was feeling the stress and pressure of house and car payments. He was frustrated by a string of bad dates, and ready to settle down in a long-term relationship. Matt was second-guessing his career decisions and contemplating a move to a new city.

He was extremely discouraged, and I asked him what had changed in his life to bring him to this crisis point. He explained that because of a shift in his family's financial well-being, his father was no longer able to bail him out if he couldn't make a payment.

Though his father had never had to help him before, Matt had always relied on his dad as a safety net. Without that safety net, Matt felt overwhelming anxiety and pressure. Since then, Matt has become accustomed to the new level of responsibility, but the transition was difficult.

GETTING INSIDE THE QUARTERLIFE CRISIS

So what causes the quarterlife crisis? Usually it isn't just one big event. Rather, it's a series of circumstances and events that compound until one issue pushes you over the edge, as happened to Matt. You may be able to live paycheck-to-paycheck in a small apartment with three roommates waiting for your big break at work, but when you add an emotional breakup, unexpected debt, a cranky boss, and a small fender bender, all within the same week, you get pushed over the edge until you can't stop asking yourself, *What the heck am I doing with my life?* A number of factors can contribute to the quarterlife crisis, including too many options, unreasonable expectations, and overwhelming stress. Here is a look at a few causes of the crisis.

Too Many Options

The sheer number of options and opportunities available to us can be overwhelming. In college, the choices were limited. On-campus or off-campus housing? Hot plate in the dorm or salad bar in the cafeteria? You could major in one of a few dozen fields. You could choose to stay in on Thursday night and watch *Must See TV* or go out with friends. Your options, which seemed unlimited compared to high school, were still pretty basic. Upon graduation, the options are virtually limitless. You can do anything.

From wedding planning to welding, and from accounting to air-traffic control, the sky is literally the limit. You can move any-where. You can work for anyone who will hire you. You can go. You can do. And the options can be downright overwhelming. The number of possibilities has the potential to both propel and para-lyze. The options can push individuals to be all that they can be, as the army says, or they can bewilder.

Holding On to the Toys "R" Us Mentality

Growing up is tough to do, and nowhere is this more apparent than in your twenties when the onslaught of adult responsibilities hits with full force. It causes many graduates to hold on to the Toys "R" Us mentality found in the company's jingle: "I don't want to grow up; I'm a Toys 'R' Us kid."

Peter, a 26-year-old native of Wyoming, says he wanted to do anything but grow up, and it caused him to spiral down after gradua-tion. "Call me Peter Pan, but I didn't want to grow up," he says. "I especially hated the idea of working for the next thirty-five or fifty years. I'd never had a job before. My parents had always encouraged me to focus on school. They kept my social life adequately funded, and I willingly complied. In their eyes, paying for dozens of movies and countless tanks of gas was well worth it. I had earned a $90,000 college education.

"I don't know if having petty jobs in high school would have improved my outlook on work. But I do know that as I wasted away my last summer before adulthood, I was bitter, resentful about the future before me, and it was eating me up inside. Work was just a product of the Fall, just a curse, right? So why should I participate? Why couldn't I break the curse?"

Peter says the day after graduation he crashed—hard. Without goals to achieve, dreams to pursue, or a career to embrace, he made a twenty-four-hour solo drive back across the country to his parents' house in Wyoming. "I rotted in my parents' basement for a couple of months," Peter recalls. "My dad occasionally encouraged me to get out, to go look for a job, to do something, but I just couldn't. I knew what was wrong. That old disdain for work had returned. It was the final showdown. If I got a job now, started a career, there'd be no going back. I'd officially be an adult, a slave, a miserable puppet in that man-eating machine, the economy. So I waited, depressed. I waited to see if my parents would ever kick me out, stop feeding me."

Fortunately, a friend stepped into Peter's life and encouraged him to take an internship at Engineering Ministries International (EMI). The friend went so far as to call the organization and express interest on Peter's behalf. Within a few weeks, Peter agreed to make the move.

Looking back on the experience, Peter describes it as the best thing that could have happened to him. "I got a global perspective that really made me appreciate all the abundance we have in the U.S., including the opportunity to try any work I want," he says. "I began to develop some vision for doing work that mattered. I glimpsed a self-identity that I could actually love. I am so much more than a dispensable cog in the economic machine."

Today, Peter works as a full-time engineer. He says that though some days he is bored and wishes he were anywhere but at work, he experiences more days when he enjoys his work and even looks forward to being at work. It's been a long journey, not without its ups and downs, but Peter says he's slowly coming to terms with being an adult.

In an effort to avoid adulthood, twentysomethings like Peter can find themselves jump-starting the quarterlife crisis in their own lives by hanging on to their childhood as long as they can.

Being on Your Own for the First Time

Everyone has a different family background. Some people have had to grow up at an extremely young age, and others have been sheltered by their parents. Depending on the amount of financial support given to you by your folks and how they chose to allow you to become an adult, decreasing the support either gradually or quickly, the challenges of facing life on your own are enough to cause you to experience the quarterlife crisis.

Sarah, a 24-year-old from Evansville, Indiana, said her parents had always been supportive of her growing up. While working at a summer camp in Woodleaf, California, she fell and broke her ankle. Her mom couldn't get on a plane to come be with her, and for the first time, she had to go through a hardship on her own. "I sat in a hospital room for two days by myself," she recalls. "I went through my first surgery alone. It was hard. I think that's the first time I realized I was an adult, and I was on my own."

Whether it is caused by a medical, financial, or relational issue, the real world catches many by surprise. Ann, a 24-year-old kindergarten teacher, describes her first year after college as the hardest of her life. "Being on my own for the first time and being away from my family and my close-knit group of friends from college have made this year a lonely one," she says. "I have learned that it is so important to have friends to encourage you."

Ann says she spent a miserable first six months in Atlanta because she was feeling sorry for herself. "I have had to learn to reach out to others and make more of an effort," she says. "I still struggle daily with thoughts of where I should live, and if I should move to a smaller city." Ann isn't alone in her struggles. Many twentysomethings struggle with living on their own for the first time and quietly wonder whether moving to a different place would make life easier.

Sometimes Life Doesn't Turn Out Like You Plan

During adolescence, it's easy to daydream about what your life will be like when you are an adult. You may be able to picture yourself getting a job, getting married, and having children. If those events don't happen according to your timetable, it can be disappointing.

Lori, a 31-year-old graduate of Cedarville University in Cedarville, Ohio, says she had a kind of calculator running in her head. "I had it all mapped out," she says. "You go to college and get married in your early twenties. If not, well, then by 25 you're married, and if not, then by 27, and if not, then you had better be married by 30 because that is a big one. But most of my friends from college got married really young. In fact, when I went back for my senior year of school, my two best friends had gotten married during the summer. At first, I thought I could catch up. Then they had their first child, and I thought I could still catch up. But by the age of 25, they'd each had their second child, and I knew I was out of the game."

Self-imposed timelines can easily weigh on twentysomethings who thought life was going to work out one way but find it going down a different path completely. The plans and goals that we had mapped out growing up are often so different from reality that if we aren't careful, the sudden changes in direction will send us into a downward spiral of doubt and anxiety.

Major-League Stress

Stress is hard to avoid. Stress is not unique to adults, but for many twentysomethings, this is the first time in life that we encounter it in such large quantities for an extended period of time.

The academic world just doesn't have the same temperature gauge as the real-world pressure cooker. As Sarah Skidmore writes, "If I had a nickel for every twentysomething I know who has broken down stressing about their jobs, life, direction or lack thereof—I would almost have enough to make a student loan payment. At one point, I lay awake almost every night filled with anxiety. I can still draw the details of the spackling on my ceiling from memory, four apartments later."[4]

Proper stress management doesn't come naturally for some twentysomethings, and a lack of training can contribute to the emotional upheaval of the quarterlife crisis. Much of the stress is self-imposed. Many twentysomethings have a list of things they want to do during their lifetime, but rather than use an entire lifetime to accomplish these things, they try to do all of them in their twenties. This notch-in-your-belt mentality causes some to travel to exotic locations, launch their own businesses, or max out their credit limits. By trying to squeeze too many accomplishments into too small a time frame, many twentysomethings find themselves exhausted—emotionally and financially.

Great Expectations

We are a generation of exceedingly high expectations. The expectations our parents place on us are nothing compared to the expectations we place on ourselves. We expect things will work out. We expect things will go our way. We expect to accomplish certain goals—which might include paying off those student loans, buying a house, getting married, or driving a Ferrari—by a certain time. When we don't meet those expectations, we are disappointed. Many of the expectations are financial. We grew up during the Reaganomics era and then the roaring 1990s with all their digital glitz and glamour. A 2001 Jobtrak study revealed that 52 percent of graduating college students expected to be millionaires by the time they were 40! Many thought (or at least hoped) there would be a nice slice of the dot-com pie left for them when it was all said and done. After the pop of the dot-com bubble, however, many of us are left with a struggling job market that has fallen and just can't seem to get back up.[5]

It's unspoken, but many twentysomethings quietly believe they should continue living the lifestyle they grew accustomed to while living under their parents' roof. They may not be able to afford the car or house their parents have, but they can buy the next model down on credit. There's a sense of entitlement woven into the expectations of what life will be like when you become an adult, and all these expectations are fulfilled at a hefty cost. Twentysomethings often are saddled with a negative credit rating as a result of acquiring too much too soon. In our desire to be successful (or at least look like it), we miss a lot of the joy that comes from living a less frantic life.

The Comparison Trap

The pressure to succeed is immense, and if it isn't coming from our parents, grandparents, or pushy members of the extended family—you know, Aunt Glenda or Uncle Max, who can't stop bragging about what your cousin accomplished when he or she was your age—it can be found among our friends as we compare and contrast our life decisions against those of our peers.

Several years ago, I took a cross-country journey to visit friends from college. It had been nearly five years since I had seen most of them, and my *I'm-coming to-visit-you-tomorrow-do-you-mind-if-I-crash-on-your-couch?* arrival was met with surprisingly warm greetings. The trip was enjoyable as I made my way up from Florida, visiting cities including Atlanta, Winston-Salem, and Washington, D.C., before heading west toward Colorado. The first friend I visited was living what I like to call the trophy life (not by biblical standards, but by worldly standards). I pulled into her driveway behind a set of matching his and her BMWs and enjoyed a night's rest in a home whose value was nearing seven digits. Not bad for someone who was only twenty-six at the time.

The rest of my friends I visited during the trip didn't own the luxury automobiles, but they were well on their way to an established adult life. A former college roommate was in the process of upgrading from a starter home to a larger one in the same neighborhood. Another friend was planning a wedding and had to decide whether to sell her home or wait for his to sell. Almost everyone I visited owned a home, a wonderful array of hip electronic devices, and oh, yeah, furniture. Furniture, of course, is the sign of someone who has it made.

Meanwhile, I was still single, cruising the country with all the earthly possessions I could possibly stuff into my six-year-old Japanese car and heading for a city I had visited only once to start a new life. I would love to say that seeing all my friends, their accomplishments, and their possessions didn't bother me and I was just thrilled for them. But it did. In fact, it sent me into a tailspin. I spent the next month second-guessing my career decisions and everything I had sacrificed to pursue my passion. I realized that it is one thing to make a sacrifice for something you love; it is a completely different thing to be confronted with what you sacrificed for the thing you love. I was reeling, and it took me nearly two months of prayer and soul-searching to fully recover and remember that what I had—a job I loved—was priceless to me. And someday I might actually own my own furniture.

Cindy, a 28-year-old living in Seymour, Tennessee, says one of her biggest challenges is not comparing her life to every other twentysomethings.' "A 25-year-old I know works for a pharmaceutical company and owns a house. A 23-year-old I know already has her master's and is looking at schools for a Ph.D. program. I am 28, and I have a friend the same age who has five children, a split-level home, seems perfectly content, and doesn't regret any of it. By now, I expected to be married, working on my Ph.D., and paying a mortgage. I live in my parents' basement, can't decide where I want to go with my education, and my job is not what I want to do with the rest of my life, let alone the next year of my life. I am surprised by not being able to figure out life and God."

When we compare where God has placed us to where He has placed our peers, we are often left second-guessing our past decisions and wondering where God is in all this mess we call our lives.

Are you feeling overwhelmed and trapped by
some of the choices you've made?

SURVIVING AND THRIVING IN THE QUARTERLIFE CRISIS

One of the keys to making it through the quarterlife crisis is recognizing that you are not alone. Twentysomethings *everywhere* are experiencing the same struggles that come with transitioning into adulthood, whether they talk about it or not. The fear, anxiety, and stress that accompany this transition can be overwhelming at times. The good news is that the crisis doesn't last forever, and if you are in the midst of a crisis right now, remember that despite what you're feeling or going through, this, too, shall pass.

Recently, I was experiencing one of those quarterlife crisis moments. I'd had a particularly stressful day that ended without resolve, and I crawled into bed exhausted and frustrated. With tear-filled eyes, I poured out my heart to God—expressing the inner aches of life. In the still darkness, I heard the faintest but clearest response: *"I am always before you."* I let those words roll over in my mind and my heart. The Creator of the universe was reminding me that He had not forgotten me. Even in the trials, even in the moments when it felt like He was many moons away, He was still near. His eyes were still on me. My struggles did not escape His notice.

And your struggles have not escaped His notice either.

So how do you survive a quarterlife crisis?

Take Responsibility for Bringing Part of the Quarterlife Crisis upon Yourself

Many people in their twenties, myself included, try to cram into ten years what it has taken every other generation twenty or thirty years to accomplish. Whether it's life experiences, travel opportunities, or financial stability, we often fall prey to putting unrealistic expectations upon ourselves. We think we can go farther and faster than previous generations. While this may be true technologically, we are burdened by more debt than the generations before us. Loans, especially student loans, are easy to get but very hard to pay back. (If for some reason you don't have one, just ask another recent grad.) The truth is that you aren't going to walk out of your parents' house and move into another one just like it unless you win the lottery, inherit a sizable chunk of change, or have some other miraculously favorable financial encounter. Cut yourself some slack.

In addition to placing unrealistic financial expectations on ourselves, we also fall prey to placing unrealistic expectations on our work. We tend to load our jobs with the burden of providing purpose and meaning in life when any job was never intended to carry such a load. Whether you're arranging flowers, ringing up sales at the Gap, or picking out blueberries for Brad Pitt, your job may seem to have little or no meaning. And that's okay. It will force you to look for life's meaning and purpose elsewhere—preferably heavenward.

Trust God

When should you trust God? When you feel panicky. When you feel easygoing. When you feel stressed. When you feel elated. When you feel depressed. When you feel excited. When you feel overwhelmed. And especially when you're facing the quarterlife crisis. Every moment—of both the hardships and the joys—is an opportunity and a choice to trust God.

I have found that in facing the quarterlife crisis and the various challenges that accompany being an adult, posture toward God is very important. I can do things on my own. I can defend myself. I can accomplish things. Or I can choose to place myself before God in humble dependence, knowing that I need Him. I am learning to lean against His breast as the disciple did at the Last Supper (John 13:23). Slowly, I am starting to wake up each morning and begin each day with the simple confession, "Lord, there is so much I need and would like to get done today, but the reality is that I can't. I need You every step of the way." I am learning to take my to-do lists, my emotional and relational needs, my heartaches and celebrations before Him, and I am finding rest in the midst of these twentysomething years.

A huge part of trusting God is being honest about how many things are outside your control. If you try to remain in control of things, you'll tend to micromanage your life and everyone else's around you in order to create a sense of stability. This is nothing but trouble!

In *How People Grow,* Dr. Henry Cloud and Dr. John Townsend write, "So many of people's problems come from trying to control things outside of their control, and when they try, they lose control of themselves. It is no wonder that praying 'the Serenity Prayer'—knowing the difference between what we can change and what we cannot—leads to people regaining control of their lives."[6]

Trusting God results in an undeniable sense of peace even in the midst of life's turbulent storms. So go ahead. Try to give it up and just trust Him.

Develop a Support System

One of the most basic needs of every human being is relation-ship. Medical studies confirm that the health of a person depends on the amount of social connection a person has with others. One study found that unmarried people with cancer have up to a 17 per-cent lower chance of survival because they receive less support than a married person.[7]

Everyone, especially those in their twenties, needs a network of people who support them. Surround yourself with people who believe in you, care for you, accept you, and love you. If you don't have this network, take steps—start attending Bible studies, join a small group, and make new friends—to establish a solid network of support. Relationships provide a foundation for a sense of belong-ing, an opportunity to care for and be cared for by others, a re-assurance of worth, assistance with problems, and guidance and advice when needed. Healthy relationships are essential, not just in your twenties, but during your entire lifetime.

Seek First the Kingdom

Jesus challenges us to first seek the kingdom of God. This com-mand sounds so easy, but it is actually really hard to do. At least a hundred other things command my attention each day. I find myself seeking money for my bank account, a CD for my music collection, and a new activity for my weekend lineup. The list goes on. Yet it's precisely in the midst of a busy schedule that Christ invites us to seek Him and His kingdom first. We are asked to put aside our busy agendas, our schedules, our demands, and our desires to seek His. It goes against our naturally self-centered desires, and yet when we choose to seek Him something wonderful happens. Our perceptions change. Our priorities change. We respond to the slight nudges of His Spirit and His leading. We become more like Him. Financial security, physical appearance, and social activities lose their prominence in our lives as He becomes preeminent in us and to those around us.

Learn How to Deal with Loss

An incredible sense of loss takes place as you enter adulthood: a loss of security, a loss of friends as you transfer to a different location, and a loss of identity. You leave a nurturing environment to enter one where "survival of the fittest" is a rule, and you go from being a person to being Employee No. 47 who is required to produce "X" amount of profit for an employer.

"You're cut loose into the real world and people put on masks to indicate that it's not a big deal," says counselor Norman Wright. "And it *is* a big deal! We're a society that hasn't been taught how to grieve. You must learn how to grieve and accept what's going on."[8]

Acknowledge there has been a loss in your life. Give yourself time to adjust and grow. And remember that God has not forgotten you. He is faithful. He will bring you through this, just as He has brought you through so many things before.

Resist Comparing Yourself to Others

Some 14-year-olds are starting their own businesses, launching their own magazines, and winning national awards. More than a handful of twentysomethings are making six figures, driving sports cars, and dating models. These are the exceptions. If you talk to their accountants, you'll find that most of them are spending money faster than they're making it and have the debt to prove it.

If you ever get these whiz kids in a quiet corner over a latte, many will tell you they're wrestling with the exact same issues you are.

Beware of people who throw off what I like to call the curve of life. Did you have a teacher in high school who graded on a curve? If everyone did poorly on a test, the grades for everyone were adjusted to higher marks. If one person did well on the exam, the curve and the grades weren't adjusted as much or, in some cases, at all. The expectation was that if one person could do well, then everyone should be able to do well. Do you know someone who made it big by the time they hit 29 (even if it was a distant cousin's friend's uncle's neighbor)? Most of us do, and these are the people who tend to throw the grading curve of life. But it's not worth comparing yourself to them, or anyone else for that matter.

No one is immune from the comparison trap, but it's worth avoiding if at all possible. There's a good old commandment about not coveting your neighbor's house, wife, servants, or ox (Exodus 20:17). The modern version of the verse tells us to avoid craving a friend's crib, spouse, techno gadgets, or set of wheels. You're only hurting yourself when you desire someone else's possessions, and with your eyes on someone else's goods, you are more likely to miss the incredible stuff you *do* have and that God has in store for you.

Develop the Skills You Need to Survive

There are about nine things I am good at—ten on a good day. That leaves about a bazillion things that I need to improve on. I have a choice. I can either panic about the fact that I don't know how to change the oil in my car, file my own taxes, thread a sewing machine, or paint a room, or I can ask for help. Sometimes asking for help requires calling on a friend or neighbor and asking for a favor. Sometimes it means surfing the Internet for an hour or subscribing to some niche magazine like *Real Simple*. Sometimes it means hiring a repairman for the garbage disposal and asking questions so you can do it yourself the next time. The good news is, it can be done. You can develop the skills you need to survive in the real world, and that usually begins with the little phrase "I need your help." You'll be amazed at how many people will respond to those four small but powerful words. Use them often.

Learn to Appreciate This Time

You're going to make mistakes. You're going to learn lessons the hard way. You're going to do things out of sequence. So what if you found your current employment at cooljobs.com, lost a few hundred (or thousand) dollars in the stock market, or signed a lease for a studio apartment you really can't afford? It's okay. Appreciate life for all its ups and downs. Remember that life is not a set of destinations but a journey. It sounds cliché, but it's still true. Despite the pressure, you don't have to know what you want to do with the rest of your life by 5 p.m. today. Allow yourself the freedom to explore. Allow yourself the freedom to make mistakes. Allow yourself the freedom to trust God with everything. Remember, if you've committed your life to Him, the ultimate destination—and the one that really counts—is already settled. So enjoy the journey. *Oh, the places you'll go!*

PHILIPPIANS 1:6

Being confident of this, that he who began a good work in you will carry it on to completion until the day of Christ Jesus.

HEBREWS 4:15–16

For we do not have a high priest who is unable to sympathize with our weaknesses, but we have one who has been tempted in every way, just as we are—yet was without sin. Let us then approach the throne of grace with confidence, so that we may receive mercy and find grace to help us in our time of need.

three

the questions that
inhabit the soul

On the outside I think I look like I have it all together . . .
or at least that's what I keep telling myself. The truth is, I
don't have it all together, as those closest to me can testify.
My lifelong friends (and, of course, my parents) know just
how much I don't have it together, and by the grace of
God, they are kind and loving to me anyway. They continue to listen patiently whenever I raise the questions
that plague my soul.

I think I had one too many late-night philosophical discussions
while I was in school. You know, the conversations where you struggle with the deeper issues of life and expose your soul until around
4 a.m. or so when either you or the person you're talking to falls
asleep on the lumpy and slightly smelly couch. I remember having

quite a few of those types of conversations during high school and college, wondering about all the possibilities out there while trying to figure out how my hopes and dreams fit into the grand scheme of things. Winning a gold medal in the Olympics. Being the first woman on Mars. Finding a cure for cancer while exploring the jungles of Africa. At 4 a.m., nothing is impossible.

Once I graduated, I didn't have nearly as much time for discussion: first, because I had to get up for work the next day, and second, because it took me a while to trust my dreams to a new group of friends with whom I could be open and honest. Questions like, *Where is God in all this? Who am I? What is my purpose? And what's really important?* began to take root in the deepest parts of my being. The problem was that they were no longer hypothetical questions for a 2 a.m. discussion over another steamed latte—they were real issues that needed real answers. Finding the answers to these questions suddenly mattered.

WHERE IS GOD IN ALL THIS?

It began with a hollow nagging. A little voice somewhere deep inside my soul started to whisper a humble but penetrating question: *Is this all there is?* I managed to squash the little voice for the first few years after college by reassuring myself that everything was just fine. I had a job (well, actually, three part-time jobs with different employers). I had a place to live (actually, that was with my parents, but it was still a roof, right?). I also had a great group of friends and a solid church, and everything in life seemed to be progressing just fine. Or was it?

Is this all there is?

The question haunted my soul.

Everything on the outside seemed fine because that's how I wanted people to see me, but on the inside I was wrestling with a sense of discontent. And I carried that bitter-tasting, unsettled feeling for some time, until I began to recognize the shadow of the longing inside me. It was an ache that all the success in the world couldn't satisfy.

In my journal, I wrote:

There is a pit hidden within my chest that science can't explain, but my body can't deny. It longs for something greater. It yearns for something more. It cries for something that it can't comprehend.

It longs for a somewhere. A something. No, it's actually a Someone. It calls out for Him.

The Him who fashioned the universe. The Him who shaped my limbs. The Him who can not only identify but also meet my most inward desires.

The Great Him. God.

At the time I wrote this, I was living the good life: attending church, reading the Bible daily, praying, tithing, fasting from time to time, and doing everything I knew from my evangelical bag of tricks to foster a vibrant relationship with God. But with all my focus on doing stuff, something, or rather Someone, was missing.

Somewhere, somehow, I had lost track of God in the busyness of day-to-day life. I was willing to meet with God in the early morning moments, but I found myself leaving Him there. God longed for me to spend time with Him, but I was busy running off to do my own thing. My convictions told me I had to start my day with God every morning, but I felt I was free to have the rest of my day to myself. I don't know how long this pattern went on—weeks or months—but I do remember waking up most mornings with hunger pains inside my soul. I needed God for more than just a quick "Hi, how's it going?" I needed Him for all the moments of the day, the successes and the failures. Without that dependence, that 24/7 relationship, the gnawing emptiness would never be satisfied.

John Fischer, author and musician, made me feel better about my internal struggle when he said that we are much better off being honest than being "Christian" because that's when God can meet us—in our honesty, rather than in our righteousness. If that means what we really need is to go scream at God, that's what we should do, and if that means being in doubt or confused, all of that is good, because that is part of the process of making our faith real. Some people perceive that struggle as a negative, but I see it as a positive.

> We are much better off being honest than being "Christian" because that's when God can meet us—in our honesty, rather than in our righteousness.

For those who have grown up in a Christian bubble—whether through homeschooling or private Christian schools and colleges—Fischer says he wishes there were a Christian world everyone could graduate into here on earth. But there isn't. "So now is a good time to think about the sloppy world we're going to live in and how we're going to walk through it, because it's not going to be easy," he says.

God Doesn't Like Cardboard

My Christian friends and I often struggle with the question, "Where is God in all this?" Certain situations bring the question bubbling up to the surface. Moving can make it challenging to find a new church or Christian community. Demands on your time can prove distracting. Accountability can slip away. Suddenly your life switches gears, and you're left alone trying to figure out how to fit God into your life. Susan, a 27-year-old graduate of Westmont University, says, "God is supposed to be the highlight of our life, and I want to live that out, but in so many ways I'm struggling to live as if He really is the highlight." I share the same struggle. Maybe you do, too.

I try to place God in all kinds of boxes. I try to box Him into my schedule. I try to box Him into a relationship. I try to box Him into thinking or responding in a certain way, blessing my behaviors, which at times He must find appalling. I place limits and expectations on a sovereign God, and it hurts my relationship with Him.

Why all the confessions about compartmentalizing? Because if I continue to compartmentalize God in my day-to-day affairs, I discover that I slowly drift away from a relationship with Him. In my mind, I never deny God or what I believe He can do. I do something far worse: I push Him over to the side so I can get things done. Sure, I allow Him to be center stage during church-related affairs and quiet times, but when church is done and the quiet time is over, I shove Him off the stage by my actions, attitudes, and behaviors and take center stage for myself.

I find myself creating opportune moments in my life for God to work and then telling Him, *Hey, don't worry—I can take it from here!* I fail to recognize that if all life is a stage, God is the director, producer, and star all at the same time. God wants to be part of every aspect of my life—a big part! I've given a polite nod to that truth for years, but now I am learning that I can't live without having God in *every* part of my life.

In order for my relationship with God to blossom, I have had to confess my boxy way of thinking and get out of His director's chair. I daily have to remember that God delights in working in ways I don't understand and frequently don't enjoy. By reading and reflecting on God's sovereignty, majesty, and power, I am slowly learning to unpack all those boxes—my cardboard misconceptions—about Him and find Him in everything and as a part of everything. I am learning to appreciate the mysterious nature of God, even the parts I can't understand. I have a long way to go.

I don't have any instant answers or twelve-step plans, but I am becoming more and more convinced that we are part of a greater story: a story that began with a Creator desiring a relationship with humankind and ends with ultimate redemption. In that story, the main character sits on a white throne in the heavens. He is incomprehensible in most regards. His power. His beauty. His awe-inspiring presence. And from that white throne, nothing goes unnoticed. The tears. The joys. The dreams. The pains. He knows it all. So whenever I find myself asking, *Where is God in all this?* I go back to the throne. No matter where I am in my relationship with

God, I can always find Him there, wanting to be with me. And whether I bow down, sit down, kneel down, or lie down, I know He will listen. So when I can't find God in my circumstances or feelings, I can always go back to what I know to be true. He has proved Himself faithful and loving, watching and guiding me.

So when the disconcerting questions—*Is this all there is?* and *Where is God in all this?*—echo inside my soul, I get rid of all the boxes of expectations, return to the throne, and spend quality time building a real relationship with a God who has it all under control.

WHO AM I?

Have you ever found yourself trapped in one of those meetings that begin with the dreaded "icebreaker"? You know, the ones where you have to furiously dart around and talk to strangers until you form a group with all the people in the room who have a birthday in the same month as yours. Or stand in front of the group and pick an adjective beginning with the first letter of your first name that describes you. That one always stumps me. I always end up introducing myself as Mango Margaret or something more ridiculous because I just can't think of anything better on the spot. It's the same way when someone says, "Describe yourself," without giving you any warning. It's something I should be able to do in a snap. After all, I hang out with myself 24/7, but somehow I always find myself kind of struggling to answer this basic question.

If you had to describe yourself in fifty words or less, what would you say?

As long as I had a little time to prepare, I would respond with something like, "My name is Margaret Feinberg, and I'm a Christian author, writer, and speaker living in Sitka, Alaska. I enjoy hiking, snowshoeing, and kayaking, and I can't get enough of the outdoors. I also like reading, listening to music, and hanging out with friends."

It's a pretty simple description, but you can already begin to formulate a picture of me in your mind. It's perfect for an icebreaker because it gives you a simple but shallow picture of my life. But the truth is that if we exchanged our descriptions, you wouldn't really know me, and I wouldn't really know you either. We are so much more than what we do or where we live. Everyone is a unique individual created in God's image. No one can be summed up in a label—whether labeled by a profession, a hobby, or a pastime—because the depth and beauty that reside in each of us go beyond these simple terms. When asked to provide others with clues about our identity, we tend to give answers that focus on what we do and end up being shallow and superficial. So let's get down to the nitty-gritty of who we really are and honestly consider the question, "Who am I?"

Who are you when no one is watching?

Who are you when all the masks and labels are removed?

Who are you *really?*

These are intimidating questions because they dig deeper into the realm of the soul than we usually dig. They are uncomfortable questions because they force us to explore aspects of ourselves we don't want to look at—let alone share with anyone else. They are necessary questions, though, because they cause us to deepen our relationship with God.

Finding Identity

Several years ago, I made a decision that I wanted to find out about God for myself. I knew what my pastor said about God. I knew what the church said about God. I knew my parents' understanding of God. And I even knew what my friends said about God, but I wanted to find out what God said about Himself. I began going through the New Testament and key books of the Old Testament, recording every verse that described a characteristic or attribute of God. It didn't take long until I had filled dozens and dozens of pages. I discovered God describes Himself as an "everlasting rock," "redeemer from of old," "a potter," "a molder," "a righteous judge," "a consuming fire," "the father of lights," and "the guardian of our soul." I learned about His likes and dislikes. During that personal time of study, I couldn't help but stand back in awe and ponder that this is the One after whom I am fashioned. I was created in His image. And He is pleased with how He created me. Everything God is, He wants to share with me. This incredible God identifies Himself with me, and He invites me to identify myself with Him. This same invitation extends to everyone.

Ephesians 1:11 says, "It's in Christ that we find out who we are and what we are living for. Long before we first heard of Christ and got our hopes up, he had his eye on us, had designs on us for glorious living, part of the overall purpose he is working out in everything and everyone" (MSG).

Our identity began with God: We were created in His image (Genesis 1:27). Our identification with God will continue into eternity. So to know our identity, we must know God. We must go to the One who created us—who knit us together in our mother's womb (Psalm 139:13)—to know who we are and who we are created to be. In order to discover our identity, we must go to God and spend time with Him, sharing the good and the bad, the laughter and the tears. Whether we run to Him or away from Him,

His desire is to be with us. Romans 12:3 says, "The only accurate way to understand ourselves is by what God is and by what he does for us" (MSG).[1]

Figuring Out Who You Are

The issue of identity is very important in our society. Christian counselor Norman Wright observes that we are no longer in a survival society as we were in the 1930s and 1940s. We've transitioned from being a survival society to becoming an identity society and asking, "What's in it for me?"[2]

So why is figuring out who you are so important? In the article "A Clear and Present Identity," Frederica Matthews-Greene writes that the question of identity is significant for Christians because we each are on a lifelong journey to find out who we really are. "We are like miners trapped at the bottom of a caved-in shaft trying to tunnel through debris to the light," she writes. "Jesus calls us toward himself, but sins and selfishness impede us. Our natural state is one of confusion. Prone to self-deception, we don't readily know which elements of self to value and which to deplore. Examination of conscience is a lost art."[3]

> The most important thing about being in your twenties isn't figuring out what you're going to do, but figuring out who you are.

Yet that examination is crucial. Writer Andy Crouch says the most important thing about being in your twenties isn't figuring out what you're going to do, but figuring out who you are. "I spent my twenties avoiding the question of what I was going to do with my life," says the 35-year-old, who spent much of his twenties apprenticing with people whom he respected. "Everything in our culture pushes people toward equating identity and activity. Who am I going to be as a lawyer or doctor? This kind of thinking ignores the most important questions such as *Who am I and what are the bedrock convictions I'm going to shape my life around?* That's what the twenties should be about and rarely are."[4]

Crouch says part of the reason it's so difficult to determine your identity after graduation is that there are so many demands on your life. Time becomes an even more valuable commodity. "There are so many new demands—just cooking for yourself and negotiating with roommates who are all outside the protective cocoon of college. It eats up a lot of time," Crouch says. "People have less bandwidth to stop and wonder—who am I becoming?"

Knowing yourself and having your identity rooted in Christ are essential because you are more than a label or a series of adjectives. You are a unique individual created with a purpose. Your identity is far more than what you do at work or in your free time. If you base your identity on these temporary things, what will happen when those things change?

Take, for example, St. Louis Rams quarterback Kurt Warner, who was originally drafted by the NFL in the early 1990s and later cut in 1994. As a young twentysomething, he found himself back doing a job that any high-school student could get. He explains the tough transition: "When I was cut from the NFL and worked in a grocery store to make ends meet, I learned about finding my identity in Christ. That's helped me remember everything I have is a gift from God."[5]

Our identities cannot be tied into what we do or our self-worth becomes a roller coaster of highs and lows, scoreboards and trophies, titles and possessions. For example, if my identity is tied into my writing, then what happens if I take a job in a different profession? Or if my identity is based on my love for outdoor activities, then what happens if I break my ankle? Who am I then?

Whether we switch jobs, get married, have children, or move to a foreign country, all of us will experience some sort of change during our lifetime. And if you're unprepared for that change, you may experience an identity crisis. In his poignant article "How I Came to Terms with My Role in the Church," Matt Woodley says that he experienced an identity crisis of sorts when he found his leadership skills questioned by the congregation he was leading. He writes, "For me, it's a short slide from 'I'm a poor leader' to 'I'm an inadequate person' to 'I'm a failure in my calling and therefore as a Christian.'"[6]

That is why it is so important to have your identity rooted in Christ. When your identity is in Him, your identity is on a solid foundation. You are no longer defined by your activities, but by the character He is developing in you. The key is to recognize Christ working in you rather than how you are specifically displaying the gifts with which He has blessed you.

Recognizing your identity in Christ requires going beyond the labels. If you work as an accountant, you probably recognize you have a gift of working with numbers. If you one day find yourself in a different profession, you can still use that same gift to balance your checkbook or help someone else by offering financial advice. If you work as a teacher, you probably have a gift of teaching. Even if a school does not employ you, you can still use that gift in raising your kids, helping a friend learn a new skill, or teaching a class at church. If you work as an assistant, whether administrative or otherwise, your gift may be that of a servant. Whenever you are serving someone at work or home, you are reflecting your true identity. Knowing who you are helps you remain balanced and healthy in all aspects of your life.

Be Yourself

I am one of those people who, when confronted with an injustice, has to speak up. When I see a wrong, I can't help but try to make it right. When there's a need, I will try to fill it, even at times to my own detriment. As I have grown in my relationship with the Lord, I am learning to season my responses with grace, love, and lots of prayer, but sometimes I wish I were someone who could just keep quiet, agree, and overlook the need.

But I can't.

I want to be an easygoing, laid-back, go-with-the-flow kind of gal, but that's not who God created me to be. Instead, I lie in bed at night thinking up crazy ways to help Mexican migrant workers, end the AIDS crisis, or start new businesses. If a discussion on any of these subjects comes up during a conversation, I'm the first to offer my two cents—or make that an entire dollar's worth—of opinions, ideas, and reflections. This is the way God made me. It is slowly being tempered with grace, maturity, and a few scraps of duct tape to help me keep my mouth shut, but I am coming to terms with the fact that God created me this way for a purpose. Who am I to say to God, the Creator of the universe, "Why did You make me this way?" (see Romans 9:20).

As I learn to understand myself and come to terms with the fact that God is still going to use me, strong will and all, for His kingdom, it gets easier to recognize what God is doing around me so I can join Him in the work He wants me to do.

Healthy Expectations

As you get to know yourself and come to terms with who you are, you also can have healthier expectations of yourself and those around you. For example, after I took a personality test and learned the four personality types, I discovered I was a highly motivated individual, which comes in handy as an entrepreneur. I also learned about other personality types, like the peacemaker and those who are naturally the life of the party.

I had a friend whom I enjoyed being around and would regularly invite to go hiking. My idea of a hike is generally a minimum of six miles, and preferably twelve, up the side of a mountain. My friend's idea of a hike was a nice half-hour walk on a flat, paved trail. After I understood our differences, I was no longer disappointed or hurt when my friend repeatedly turned down my invitations for a long hike. What I viewed as relaxing and enjoyable, she perceived as grueling and exhausting. And that's okay. When we hang out now, I choose less-stressful activities like watching a movie or grabbing a bite to eat. Our relationship is stronger because I know myself better and how to relate to her in a healthy way.

Having your identity in Christ helps strengthen relationships by removing false expectations and misconceptions. You can be more confident in your friendships because your security is rooted in an eternal foundation. The apostle John realized this. When you look through the book of John, you'll soon realize that John calls himself "the disciple whom Jesus loved." What a foundation for identity. The amazing thing is that what is true for John is true for us as well. Having your identity rooted in Christ will erase unhealthy thinking patterns and affirm your true worth and value. As Dr. Neil Anderson says, "The more you reaffirm who you are in Christ, the more your behavior will begin to reflect your true identity!"[7]

Gifts and Weaknesses

As followers of Christ, we are called to use the talents and gifts with which God has entrusted us. But how can we use them if we don't know what they are? By knowing our strengths, we can put our talents and gifts into action. The body of Christ and the church can function properly when everyone is using his or her gifts. For example, when I take spiritual gift tests, one of the qualities that rise to the top is hospitality. It doesn't come as any surprise to those who know me. I naturally love having people over for dinner, throwing parties, and organizing social events. One of my favorite holidays is Thanksgiving. So throughout the year, I'll throw informal Thanksgiving dinners—complete with turkey, gravy, mashed potatoes, stuffing, and pie—and invite a dozen or so people over for a feast.

All that to say, when I realize that one of my gifts is hospitality, I can use that gift to help build relationships among believers and nonbelievers. I can be intentional. I can try to prepare my home so it's always available for guests and use my strength—hospitality—to bless others.

As you reflect on the different aspects of your identity, you may discover you also have been basing your self-worth on things that are contrary to God's Word. You may feel or think things about yourself that aren't true. You may notice yourself trusting in things or people other than God. You may find your identity resting in worldly accomplishments or material possessions. I've done some reflecting on these issues and have discovered that while it's a painful process to question and discover what I'm trusting in (and it's not always God), it's a very necessary aspect of growing in a relationship with Jesus Christ.

Unfortunately, the hardest part of knowing yourself is knowing your weaknesses. Everyone likes to focus on what they're good at or what they like, but knowing one's weaknesses is important. Several years ago, I went through a Bible study that asked the question, "What causes you to sin?" I had never thought about the trigger points of my sinful behavior. I spent some time evaluating possible answers. I could walk by a drug dealer on the street and not think twice about making a purchase. I could pass a magazine stand of pornography and not have the temptation to take a peek. I could drive by a bar and resist its potentially wild impulses. What I discovered was pretty eye-opening. What causes me to sin is one of the simplest things of all: lack of sleep.

When I don't get enough sleep, I get cranky. I am short with people. I get impatient. I tend to snap at people and situations that are really very simple to handle. Lack of sleep heightens my sinful nature, so I am more judgmental, harsh in my responses, and more likely to overeat. A simple thing like lack of sleep heightens my ability to sin.

Once I realized this pattern in my behavior, I decided to take steps to avoid it. I could excuse myself from a dinner party or get together earlier without any guilt. I now know that I have to make wiser choices with my time. And I have figured out that it's essential to give myself at least two mornings a week when I can sleep in as late as possible and give my body the opportunity to recover. When I choose to be honest about my weaknesses, I can make more responsible decisions and choose to make changes in areas of my life that will really make a difference.

◎   ◎   ◎

Our generation is not content being just another gear in the system. Each of us desires to be recognized as someone unique, with individual gifts and value. Figuring out who you are is extremely important for yourself, your relationships with others, and your personal relationship with God. Answering the question, "Who am I?" begins with asking yourself some very basic questions. *What do I like? What do I dislike? What are my talents? What are the things I'm not so good at? How do I relate to others? What kind of people am I attracted to? What kind of people do I tend to avoid?*

> Our generation is not content being
> just another gear in the system.

A number of resources are available to help you better understand yourself, and I highly recommend taking advantage of them. One of the biggest helps I've found is to take a personality test. A variety of them are available including the Myers-Briggs Type Indicator (MBTI), the DiSC Personal Profile System (PPS), the Biblical Personal Profile (BPP), the LaHaye Temperament Analysis (LTA), and the Personality Profile Test (PPT).[8]

Even if you took one of these tests while you were in high school or college, it is a good idea to take one again. As individuals, we are constantly growing, developing, and changing. Some of the traits you had a few years ago may have gotten stronger or faded away to nothing. One friend of mine says she took personality tests in high school and college, but it wasn't until she took the test a couple of years out of college that the results were helpful. She admits that when she was younger she would fill out the responses on the test based on who she wanted to be or who she thought she wanted to be rather than who she was. If used properly, these tests can be very helpful in getting to know yourself.

In addition, tests that identify your talents and gifts can be useful, too. A variety of tests, including the Spiritual Gifts Inventories (SGI) and the Career Direct Guidance System, is available. I highly recommend taking more than one of these, because each test has different strengths and weaknesses. Also, taking different tests will help confirm or deny certain patterns.

Friends provide another valuable resource for discovering your identity. I am speaking of friends who are *true* friends—ones who are healthy, supportive, loving, and promote healthy behavior, not the guy you know from the break room at work. Often it's a friend who will point out a talent or strength you didn't know you had and encourage you to use it more often. True friends can also lovingly warn you of weaknesses or destructive patterns of behavior. If you want to get together with a friend and go over the results of a personality test, I highly recommend it. There's nothing like an honest friend to confirm whether the test results are accurate or completely off base.

Your real identity comes from perceiving and understanding yourself as God does. That's the ultimate reality. It's based around real truth and not just perceptions. If you want to know who you are, you need to place yourself before God, complete with all of your dreams, hopes, fears, and failures, and ask Him to make sense of it all. Ask God, "Who am I?" and listen for a response.

THE IMPORTANCE OF KNOWING WHO YOU ARE

→ It helps you have peace with yourself.

→ It helps foster healthy relationships with others.

→ It helps you use your strengths.

→ It helps you know your weaknesses.

WHAT IS MY PURPOSE?

Everyone is driven by something. What drives you? At your very core, a sense of purpose should drive or compel you toward something. But where are you headed? And, more important, what is really pushing you in that direction?

The Westminster Confession tells us that the chief aim of man is to know God and enjoy Him forever. It's a wonderful definition of life's purpose, but for those who have wrestled with the issue of purpose for any length of time, it can seem like just another pat Sunday school answer. Don't get me wrong: The Westminster Confession is biblical and true. The Bible reminds us that *"everything* got started in him and finds its purpose in him" (Colossians 1:16 MSG). Dan Kimball, author of *The Emerging Church,* says that no matter what you do—whether you're a landscape architect, high-school teacher, stay-at-home parent, or employee at Home Depot—God wants to be in a deep relationship with you. That relationship between you and God will impact the relationships you have with other people in more ways than you could ever imagine.

"That means that if you're working at McDonald's, you now have fifteen coworkers and you can be Jesus to them," Kimball says. "You can hang out with them, and hopefully Christ will be seen in you."[9]

God has given you the task and mission of making Him known to others. The Great Commission isn't just for pastors and missionaries; it is for each of us who believes that Christ died to save us personally and redeem humankind globally. Recognizing your purpose—to know God, to enjoy Him, and to represent Him—breathes life into the mundane existence this life can become.

Your purpose goes far beyond what you do, whom you marry, or where you live. When your purpose becomes your primary mission, the focus of your activities will change. This is illustrated by an old story told about a foreman who asked one of the builders on his site what he was doing. "I'm breaking rocks," he replied. When he posed the question to a second worker, he responded, "I'm earning for my family." And when he asked a third worker, he responded, "I'm building a cathedral."[10] Indeed, knowing your purpose, which is rooted in eternity, will change your perspective on everything you do.

WHAT'S REALLY IMPORTANT?

What's really important in life? It's a simple question. If you take out a sheet of paper and a pen and set a timer for ten or fifteen minutes, you can probably create a fairly extensive list. As you reflect on what is truly important to you, though, some of the items will rise to the top of the list while others drop to the midpoint or even lower.

It's one thing to know your priorities, but it's another and much more difficult thing to actually live them out day to day. Demands pile up. Schedules fill. Voices cry out. Somewhere between the grocery list, the to-do list, and the countless receipts you're saving for the budget you promised you'd start two months ago, the list of priorities gets forgotten or at least misplaced. The precious is exchanged for the necessary.

My parents told me, "You can have what you want, but you just can't have *everything* you want." I'm still learning that lesson. Prioritizing is one of the biggest challenges in my life right now. I know what I believe is important. But putting my beliefs into action and living with the consequences can be extremely difficult. Let me give you an example. I believe in tithing. I totally agree that I should give the first fruits of my income to God. But it's hard to write the check. To take it to another level, it's even more challenging to write a check when you're not sure whether you're going to have enough money to pay rent, car insurance, and the electric bill—and still eat.

I've realized that I can choose to tithe or I can buy what I want with the extra cash. I can do one or the other, but I can't do both (without a credit card). The decision to tithe will cost me. I may have to choose to stay home when all my friends are going to the movies or out to dinner. It means missing a sale on some cool jeans or waiting another two weeks to buy that CD or book I want from amazon.com. Every decision I make has consequences, even when they are good decisions. What I choose reflects my priorities, and each little choice adds up to a lifestyle. As I grow, my priorities are constantly shifting, as I'm sure yours are, too.

My college friend Linda met her husband, Greg, while spending a year abroad in Germany. When they first returned to the United States, they moved into her parents' guesthouse—a six-hundred-square-foot home divided into five tiny rooms. "We had little income and literally did not buy meat or cheese except for special occasions, and otherwise lived as paupers," she recalls. "When we finally bought Greg a car, we spent $1,500 on a nine-year-old Toyota Camry and did so only after having everything checked out. We felt that we were really stretching to make the purchase. I remember one night when we had planned to splurge and go to dinner and a movie, and I ended up in tears because I was so worried about money, I felt guilty and irresponsible about spending so frivolously."

Four years later, Greg and Linda purchased their first home: a five-thousand-square-foot home located on a 4.5-acre parcel of land. "We're no longer cramped for space, and it feels great," Linda says. "On the other hand, the financial burden I have put on my shoulders feels very heavy sometimes. The stress of continuing to do what I do to pay the bills, cover the mortgage, and maintain this life we have created can be overwhelming. This, of course, takes us back to the issue about priorities. I see how people can feel very trapped by their lives. I could not give up my job, be a stay-at-home mother, work in public service, volunteer full-time, work at something I feel passionate about, get a long-term illness or injury, or in any way allow our household income to drop significantly without having to make some major changes, including selling our home. Funding our lifestyle is just as much my job as it is his."

Linda says she often wonders about couples where the wife

doesn't work or the husband makes all the decisions and bears all the responsibility for everything except clothes, dinner, cleaning, and children. "What must that be like?" she wonders. "Some days, I think I have created this monster, and now I have to feed it or get rid of it lest it eats me, and it makes me feel tired. Finding balance is tough. There is so much to balance—the now or the later, the vacation fund or the retirement fund, getting ahead at work or working on my marriage, owning a home I love or being owned by a home that must be cleaned and stained and furnished, seeing the world or having a profession."

As Linda's choices demonstrate, it is hard to establish priorities and easy to lose sight of them under the pressures of day-to-day life. Depending on the choices we make, it can be increasingly difficult to live our lives according to priorities.

God-Centered Priorities

As we covered earlier in this chapter, the priority of the Christian life, first and foremost, is to follow your purpose/primary mission: to know God and enjoy Him. The Creator already knows us and desires to be known. The more you know God, the more you understand His will and can prioritize your life according to His will, rather than according to the expectations of those around you. There are plenty of people around you who would love to make decisions for you. But it is you and your relationship with God, not those people, that will either grow or suffer because of your choices.

Living your life according to God-centered priorities takes discipline. It also requires knowing your limitations. In case you haven't figured it out by now, you can't do everything.

HOW DO YOU KNOW YOU'RE DOING TOO MUCH?

○ You show up late to events.

○ You go to bed exhausted almost every night and wake up exhausted most mornings.

○ You regularly double-book yourself for meetings and events.

○ Your friends don't know if you're really going to show up.

○ You don't have any time to relax on a regular basis.

○ You wake up with a to-do list playing in your mind.

○ You can't do what you feel compelled to do because you're already committed to something else.

○ You don't have time for new friends, let alone the ones you have.

I can ask this because I've done each one of these things at one time or another—or like right now, when I'm doing all of them at once. I regularly fall into the trap of overcommitting. I commit to attending four or five events during the week, and then get mad at myself when I'm exhausted and still have to go. I am still in the process of learning God-centered prioritizing. I am learning to pray before committing to events—even when it's as simple as a dinner engagement with family or volunteering a few hours at church. I am learning not to give the knee-jerk response of "Sure, I'd love to!" and instead to pause and reflect on my schedule for the week. *Am I already overcommitted? Do I really have the time? Is saying yes going to put my life on a treadmill that's already going too fast?*

I am learning the most powerful word for avoiding over-commitment. It has only two letters: *n-o*. Of course, writing *no* and actually saying no to a person who has a real need or a person you want to impress are two very different things. I have also found that opening up my life to a mentor or trustworthy friend is helpful. Asking for input from people you trust is crucial in helping you live out your priorities. When I am in the middle of a busy week, I often can't discern what is important, but someone who doesn't have to live my schedule can. I am also discovering that it's actually not a bad thing to do less. When my schedule is less busy, I find that I am more available to be used by God. Those needs I once interpreted as interruptions to my schedule—a person who needs a ride to the airport or someone who stops by so they don't have to be alone— are welcomed into my life as opportunities to serve and love others because I have the time. What a difference a little freedom in your schedule can make in helping to glorify God!

I am also learning that the bottom line of prioritizing is that I don't add something to my schedule unless I make a genuine commitment to take out something else. That may mean watching less Comedy Central, unplugging the Xbox, or turning off the computer instead of surfing the Net until all hours of the morning. It may mean stepping down from leadership positions in the church and letting someone else have the opportunity to lead. This is what it takes for me; you probably have different things in your life that would need to change.

Rich Hurst, coauthor of *The Quest for Christ,* notes that to do less, you have to feel good about yourself. You have to make choices about what is truly important and invest in what matters, as illustrated in the story of the talents found in Matthew 25:14–30. "If you dance for everyone, you will feel no one's love," Hurst says.[11]

A good part of prioritizing is learning how to rest. Our upwardly mobile, fast-paced society has a rhythm that demands rest. It is hard to remember that the downbeat is healthy. Over the last few years, I've been learning the importance of taking a Sabbath—at least one day—to rest. Some weeks the day I take off from work changes, but I've found that God honors this simple discipline. When I rest one day, the other six become more productive. I can get more done in my job and give more in my relationships.

Slowly, I am learning how to establish priorities. I can't do everything, but I am learning that if I make wise choices with God's leading, the few things that I commit to, I am able to do well.

◎   ◎   ◎

The twentysomething years are a critical time when you start to stake your claim on the piece of reality in which you're going to invest your life. Immerse yourself in the Word of God while surrounding yourself with people who love you, and this period of your life will be a lot less stressful. These next few years are a time to sort through issues of purpose, identity, and what's important—and as you do, you can launch into a life that really matters.

FAST FACTS

→ The Ball and Chain of Debt: In 1999–2000, 64 percent of students graduated with student loan debt. The average student loan debt was $16,928. ("The State PIRG's Higher Education Project," www.pirg.org/highered/highered.asp?id2=7947.)

→ All in the Family: Sixty percent of college students plan to move home after graduation. ("To Be About to Be," *American Demographics,* September 2003.)

→ Lack of Faith in Social Security: A survey of 18- to 34-year-olds by Oppenheimer Funds found that 84 percent of respondents favor giving workers a choice of where to invest their Social Security taxes. Some 53 percent think they will outlive Social Security. (Elsa C. Arnett, "Generation X-ers Indifference Could Cost Them More Than They Think," Knight Ridder/Tribune News Service, January 27, 1999.)

four

the questions that
press us forward

As if all the identity questions stirring around inside me aren't enough, I also have the practical questions that still need to be dealt with. I am constantly wondering, *What is coming around the next corner?* No one can tell me. So I've got to learn to wait patiently and still be ready to move at the same time—neither of which I do very well.

One of my best friends, Scotty, works only two days a week during the winter months. He snowboards the other five. By choosing to live on less and enjoy life more, he has created a lifestyle around his passion—snowboarding. How does he do it? He lives simply. He drives old, used cars with lots of character. He shops at Wal-Mart. He resists the urge to be a mindless consumer: He makes purchases based on his actual needs rather than what society tells him he needs.

Scotty has also found jobs that support his lifestyle. He works as a taxi driver two days a week, where he earns a reasonable hourly wage plus some nice tips. Then he spends the other five days a week on the slopes. During the last few summers, Scotty has worked on a trail maintenance crew for the U.S. Forest Service. He loves the outdoors, and his work satisfies his hunger for hiking, camping, and enjoying nature. More recently, Scotty began working at a world-class golf course so he would have free access to the greens. Talk about loving your work!

Scotty and I have different passions. His are snowboarding and nature. Mine are writing and God. Yet through his lifestyle choices, Scotty has shown me what it means to live life according to your passions. He has made the sacrifices and life choices that enable him to do what he wants to do. He had to give up a nice apartment and a cool car, but he has gained a lifestyle that anyone in a cubicle would envy. I look at my life and think about how I should be making more of the sacrifices and life choices necessary to do what I am created to do. Yet figuring out these issues isn't a snap. I find myself wrestling with questions of vocation, calling, and career.

Just when you think you're getting settled into your twenties, some of the same questions you thought you had answered return for a second round. You can try to avoid them. You can try to ignore them. You can even try keeping yourself busy enough to pretend they don't really exist. But even after entering the real world, most twentysomethings wake up one morning and wonder, *What the heck am I doing with my life?*

WHAT THE HECK AM I SUPPOSED TO DO WITH MY LIFE?

Kristen, a 25-year-old high-school teacher, says she is still trying to figure out what to do with her life. "I thought a four-year degree from a university would mean something more, and instead I got a job making $11 an hour," she says. "I feel that our generation is different from our parents' in that they went to college to study 'X,' and then they graduated with a degree in 'X,' got a job doing 'X,' and at 55 retired from their job doing 'X.' In our generation, we enter college not entirely knowing what we want to do, and then graduate still not knowing!"

The question of schooling and finding a job becomes particularly complex for Christians trying to figure out their spiritual calling and earthly career all at the same time.

Going Splat on the Mission Field

Like Kristen, I graduated from college with no idea what I wanted to do with the rest of my life, and worse, I had no idea what God wanted me to do. Somewhere in my religious upbringing, well-meaning church members and leaders had instilled in me the idea that some professions make God happier than others. I came to believe that people who really loved God were either in full-time ministry or on the mission field. Since my first choice—Princeton Theological Seminary—rejected my application, I figured missions was the next best way to do what God would want me to do. Wrong.

After my summer internship in Florida, I boarded a plane for Tegucigalpa, Honduras, for a weeklong missions trip. The week went so well that I decided to stay and help a local family establish a water system in an outlying village. I wish I could tell you that during the two months that followed, I was able to verbally share the gospel and touch lives and became radically transformed by the experience. But I can't. As a matter of fact, that is far from the truth. We didn't have a vehicle to get to the village, so I rarely left the house. Instead, I found myself living with a local family, eating the food placed before me, and getting increasingly ill. I was bedridden, or rather bathroomridden, for weeks. Dizzy spells, fainting, and nausea accompanied what the doctors finally determined was an "amoeba"—some little bug that loves to grow in the stomachs of foreigners.

A full month later when I was feeling better, I ventured out of the house on my own. On the bus ride home from a nearby city, a man held an eight-inch steel knife against my throat (it might as well have been a machete) and demanded that I give him my stack of luggage. For a few truly *Dumb and Dumber* moments, I tried to say no and fight him off with a water bottle. Finally, in a brief moment of sanity, the words of my father ran through my mind: *If you're ever being robbed, give them what they want. It's never worth it.* I handed him my bags. Everything was taken except for my passport, $82, and some spare change. In spite of the toilet hugging and robbery, I was still clinging to the idea of being a missionary. Over the next month or so, the hardships of being away from family and friends, the constant battle with sickness, and the effects of culture shock finally helped me realize that it was time to go home.

But after being back in the States only a short time, I began to wonder if I had given up too soon. I was second-guessing my decision and questioning whether I had just let the hardship get to me. If I really loved God, then wouldn't I want to serve Him on the mission field? So I saved some more money and returned to Honduras. Though the second visit was less traumatic, I lasted less than a month and returned home reeling from the experience. I felt like a failure. It took me two months to come to terms with the fact that I was not called or even cut out to be a missionary. What God wanted me to do and what I thought He wanted me to do were two completely different things.

The story of Jesus speaking to Peter in the Gospel of John was instrumental in helping me get a grip on the reality that God has different plans for different people. In the final portion of John 21, after Jesus serves a surprise breakfast to some of His disciples on the beach, He addresses the feisty, ambitious disciple Peter. He asks Peter the famous question, "Do you love Me?" three times before He makes a prophetic observation about Peter's future:

> When you were young, you were able to do as you liked and go wherever you wanted to; but when you are old, you will stretch out your hands and others will direct you and take you where you don't want to go. (John 21:18 TLB)

John goes on to tell the reader that Jesus was informing Peter of the kind of death he would die to glorify God. It was a heavy-handed prophetic message. Most of us would rather not know how we are going to die, and Peter was no exception. Jesus concluded this encounter with the two-word command "Follow Me."

Reading this passage, I felt an eerie silence inside my soul. Christ was speaking to Peter, but He also was speaking to me: *Follow Me.* I realized these two words were a challenge for me as well. The calling was simple and to the point, and I wasn't supposed to add to God's calling for me with words like "to Honduras" or "to the mission field." I was simply to follow Him. The eternal call of Christ on our lives is not to a particular person, place, or position here on earth, but rather to a deepening relationship with Him. Though at times, people, places, and different job positions will manifest themselves as part of that call, the heart is to be a follower of Jesus Christ. That's it. Pretty simple, but pretty hard to live out.

> The eternal call of Christ on our lives is not to a particular person, place, or position here on earth, but rather to a deepening relationship with Him.

It should come as no surprise that the majority of passages in the New Testament that speak of calling have little to do with professions. The apostle Paul, who refers to the word *calling* the most, uses it in terms of salvation. This calling is high or upward (Philippians 3:14), it is heavenly (Hebrews 3:1), and it is holy in its aim and focus (2 Timothy 1:9). In Ephesians 4:1–3, Paul encourages, "As a prisoner for the Lord, then, I urge you to live a life worthy of the calling [or *salvation*] you have received. Be completely humble and gentle; be patient, bearing with one another in love. Make every effort to keep the unity of the Spirit through the bond of peace."

Paul urges us to pursue humility, gentleness, patience, and love before we set our hearts and minds on a particular profession, even one involving some type of ministry. The primary Christian calling is heavenward. We are called to be like Christ. We are also called to know the One who is calling. To know the Savior should be our highest goal and the focus of our lifetime here on earth. I have learned that just as the sacred can be made secular with the wrong attitudes, the secular can be made sacred with the right ones. The key is to look for God's handiwork in everything you do—whether delivering a pizza, writing a memo, or counseling a child.

Of course, while we are seeking God with our hearts and minds, that sense of calling affects everything we do on earth. Despite heavenly longings, most of us will find ourselves living out a forty-hour (or more) workweek, paying bills, and keeping the creditors at bay. Most of us will struggle to figure out what God wants us to do with the twenty-four hours He gives us each day.

You may have prayed a hundred times, "God, just tell me what to do, and I'll do it." But all you hear is silence. You keep asking the question, "What am I supposed to do with my life?" If that's you, and you are still searching and trying to figure out what you're supposed to do with your life, don't stop asking God for direction. If you've asked a hundred times, ask a hundred more. Keep seeking Him. Remember that life is not a job title or position; it's a journey in growing in relationship with Him. And that journey may take you into a profession or a place and fulfill dreams and desires you've never even considered or dared to share with anyone else.

Searching for My Place in This World

Believe it or not, there are small groups of twentysomethings who actually know what the heck they are going to do with their lives professionally. The strangest fact about these individuals is that they have been aware of it for years. Whether they stumbled upon it by chance in school, have known it since childhood, or inherited a family business, they know their career direction. For some, a hardship or struggle may have caused them to enter a particular profession so they could help others. A special gifting may have made it obvious to everyone around them that they would pursue a particular course of study. Whatever the cause, these individuals have always had an answer when they were asked, "What are you going to be when you grow up?" And now, twenty years later, they're sticking to it.

The vast majority of us are still searching for a niche. We have an idea of some things we're good at, but we're still trying to figure out what makes us tick and exploring all the options to find out what we're supposed to do. A job may pay the bills, but a hunger for satisfaction and fulfillment plagues the soul. Some people honestly have no idea what they want to do with their lives. No particular career, profession, or field makes the heart sing.

If you don't know what you want to do with your life, keep trying and test the waters in a whole new way. Sign up with a local school district and try substitute teaching. You don't need a degree in education to substitute teach in most public-school systems, and you may discover something you enjoy. Ask friends and family members if you can shadow them at work for a day. Pick up a few part-time jobs. Consider temp jobs in order to explore the landscape of professions. Remember that discovering what you *don't* want to do is extremely helpful. Marking the really terrible jobs off the list definitely gives me a feeling of satisfaction. Plus, the stories are always good for a laugh. Here are a few things to remember in your search for a career:

You don't have to do anything forever. Don't be afraid of trying new professions. You don't have to do them forever. The age of working for the same company for an entire lifetime has passed. Companies now expect you to move on, and they are redesigning their benefits packages to meet the increasing number of mobile workers.

Go into a new job (whether it's temporary or permanent) with your eyes wide open. When you're in a new job—even if it's one you don't particularly like—take time to analyze the situation. What do you enjoy about the job? What do you dislike about the job? Are there any similarities about the things you appreciate or despise when comparing it to previous jobs? Maybe you prefer more responsibility? Maybe you enjoy less structure? Maybe you want to be creative at work? Maybe you prefer working with fewer people? Maybe you excel at motivating, teaching, managing, or analyzing? Use each of your job experiences to learn more about yourself and your talents.

You don't have to live in the box of "traditional work." The nine to five may not be for you. It wasn't for me. I wanted to fit in, really, I did. The draw of a steady income, health benefits, and job security was extremely appealing, but in the end, I felt trapped by the cubicle walls. I suppose everyone does to some degree, but some people thrive in a structured environment like a plant in the sun. I just wilt.

When I was inside my cubicle, I didn't want to go up the corporate ladder; I just wanted to get out. I felt like I was dying inside. That may seem a little dramatic, but while everyone else was busy figuring out how to land a promotion or get assigned to some special project, I was daydreaming about using a chain saw to carve my own window to the outside world like a character in some "Dilbert" comic strip. While others were putting in extra hours, I was the first one out the door—without any guilt, I might add. Instead of enjoying lunch with coworkers, I was out jogging—even when the temperature topped one hundred degrees—just to be able to enjoy the outdoors.

I am not meant for the big-city, corporate world, and that's okay. Maybe you're not built for it either. The good news is, thousands of jobs today don't involve cubicles or commutes. A growing number of businesses can be developed in your own home. Whether you are in sales, marketing, promotion, or journalism, you can work from home and still be successful. You can also start your own niche business, whether it's on the Internet, walking dogs, or house sitting—all without a cubicle. However, be aware that freedom doesn't come without a cost. Uncle Sam will try to take an extra 15.5 percent of your income if you're self-employed, and no one will be handing out health benefits or a pension plan. But it just might work for you, so don't settle for the cubicle till you at least try it.

You can do what you like to do. In case no one has told you yet, it is possible to actually get paid to do what you enjoy doing. You may not make a fortune. You may never be famous. You may only be able to afford to do it part-time. But you can do it. You can earn an income, modest as it may be, from what you enjoy doing. Maybe you like painting, singing, sculpting, drawing, or cooking. You can either sell your talent or use it to tutor or teach others. Depending on the income from your full-time job, you may even be able to do what you love for free. It may not be full-time, but for at least part of the time, you'll get to do what you love.

Remember that whatever you decide to do will probably change. You probably will have a different job title in a few years and eventually switch companies or your career goals. You may start out as a high-school teacher and discover you would prefer to teach college courses. Or you may start as an office assistant and realize your passion is cooking. Your desires, interests, and needs will change in the years to come. So remember to be flexible and willing to try new things. My friend Beau was working as a dorm counselor at a boarding school for high-school students. When the school year ended, he found a job at a local jewelry store that happened to pay well. While working at the store, he not only discovered he loved working in sales, he also found he had a knack for working with jewelry. Beau's boss recently told him that he is picking up basic jewelry skills faster than anyone he's seen over the last two decades. Beau is now considering studying to be a jeweler. You never know what summer job or part-time position may lead to a new profession.

CAN I REALLY DO IT?

God has a plan for my life, even if it isn't in full-time missions work. I had to remind myself of this truth after I returned from my failed attempts to be a missionary in Honduras. So I began praying, asking God what I should do with my life, or rather with the life He had given me. I prayed for nearly two months and didn't hear a peep.

At the time, I was living at home, and fortunately my parents were very gracious about my lack of vocational direction. I was picking up odd jobs—as a ski instructor, part-time nanny, and kids adventure camp counselor—to pay for my other expenses. Those job titles were the kind that made my fellow college graduate friends jealous. A day spent hiking outdoors or hitting the slopes always beat a day in the office in terms of enjoyment, even if it couldn't compete in the paycheck department.

I knew, or at least hoped, that God had something for me beyond being a ski bum for the rest of my life, so I continued to pray. At the time, it seemed it wasn't doing any good. I asked myself a rather simple question:

> If I could do anything with my life,
> assuming that money and time were no
> object, what would I choose to do?

I thought about this question for less than ten seconds, and I knew the answer: I wanted to write. In the deepest part of my being, I longed to write. I didn't even care what I wrote. I just wanted to write. Knowing the answer, I had to ask myself the natural follow-up question:

> What is stopping me from doing it?

This question was a lot more difficult to answer. I pulled out a sheet of paper and began recording my responses. My contacts in publishing were extremely limited. I had only a handful of published samples from my internship. I didn't know how to approach new magazines, or if they would even consider me. I didn't have a laptop. It would take months or maybe even years to build up a business.

The list kept getting bigger and bigger.

I realized this was going to be a very difficult decision to make. Then the really hard issues began to surface. I was afraid of failing. I was afraid of rejection. I was afraid the whole thing wouldn't work, and I'd be right back where I started. The fears and reasons stacked up higher and higher.

But when I reflected on the first question, about what I really wanted to do, I realized that my desire to do what I loved was greater and more powerful than all the reasons I could come up with not to do it. A battle raged inside me, but in the end, the compelling desire to write was greater than my insecurities.

I told my parents I was going to begin writing. They were supportive and invited me to live at home with them as long as I needed. I headed to the library and checked out a stack of books on publishing. Most were discouraging. They quoted dismal statistics on the odds of first-time writers getting published. I knew I didn't have much of a chance, but I decided to contact a half-dozen different Christian magazines anyway and ask if I could write for them. All but one said yes, and I knew God had opened some very special doors for me.

Those doors have continued to open over the last six years. Hundreds of magazine articles and more than a half-dozen books later, I have found my niche. I have found the place into which God wants me to pour my life. It isn't Honduras, but the written word. I wish I would have found it earlier. I wish I had a journalism degree to back up my efforts, but I don't, and it makes me all the more reliant on God.

People have asked me how I know that I'm supposed to write. How do I know it's my calling? I feel the holy hum of God's presence when I write. Some days I feel like Jesus pulls up a chair beside me as I prod the keyboard with ideas and phrases. Some days I can't help but stop and worship God for all He has allowed me to do. Joy abounds in my work. When I write, I get to experience joy that wells up from the innermost parts of my being and overflows onto paper.

Some days are hard. Some days the words don't flow. Some days are spent aligning footnotes with the text, and I'd rather be at the dentist having a root canal than fine-tuning a manuscript, but the great days make it all worth it. When you find your niche, joyfulness builds up inside you, even when the job is not fun or easy. Now I will ask you this potentially life-altering question:

> If you could do anything with your life, assuming that money and time are no object, what would you choose to do?

Quickly, now: What is your response? What would you choose to do with your life?

> If I could do anything, I would _____.

Does the answer surprise you? Or has it been tucked away in your heart all along? I've asked hundreds of people this question, and almost everyone has an answer. Their eyes usually light up and their face softens as they share what they'd really like to be doing. Sometimes the answers are funny, strange, or even shocking. I've talked to doctors who really want to be teachers, firefighters who want to be astronauts, and artists who want to be dog groomers. I met one highly successful accountant who told me with an unmistakable glimmer in her eye that she had always wanted to be a truckdriver!

What is surprising is how few people are actually doing what they feel compelled to do. The reason is usually linked to the follow-up question:

> What is stopping you from doing what you want to do?

Practical reasons may top the list. Debt and financial limitations. The demand for additional schooling. You may have a spouse or children to support. The reasons are varied and endless. Deeper concerns, including fear, pride, and expectations, may choke out the desire, too.

Some of these concerns are valid. If you have a newborn, it probably isn't the time to start a business that requires you to be away for weeks at a time. If you have heavy debt, you need to consider paying it off before going out on a financial limb. You always need to assess the practical roadblocks and consider the spiritual ones, too.

When I asked Leif, a 26-year-old employee of the federal Transportation Security Administration (TSA), what he would like to do with his life, he didn't hesitate: "I want to fly!" he exclaimed.

"Do you want to fly planes, gliders, helicopters, or something else?" I asked.

"I don't care," he answered. "I would be happy in any or all of them; I just want to fly."

When I asked what was stopping him from pursuing his dream, he said that he has thought and prayed about it often, but he feels God is telling him to wait on Him with that desire and continue in his current profession with airport security. He is right! He shouldn't drop everything and head to flight school, especially if God hasn't told him to go.

The Compelling within You

You may not have such an obvious answer to give. You have a dream, a desire, something within your being that makes you want to do something. You can't quite explain it, and in many regards it doesn't even sound logical. It's what I like to call a *compelling*. You are being compelled to do something. You can go along in your daily grind until you stumble onto something that reminds you of your compelling, and then you think, *Yeah, that's what I would really like to be doing.*

Maybe it's something that doesn't require a career change; it just requires a shift in your schedule or use of free time. Maybe you feel compelled to work with the homeless, AIDS patients, or hospice patients. Maybe you feel compelled to tutor, mentor, or teach Sunday school. Maybe you feel compelled to start a new ministry at your church. Whatever it is, you feel compelled.

Or maybe it is something that requires a change in profession. It may take some additional classes, an additional degree, or a business plan. You know the things that are standing in your way. There will always be a few, but are those things greater than the compelling within you? Has God been leading you toward doing something new and you've missed those gentle nudges?

Why is this important? Because God, more than anyone else, knows who you would be at your best. He knows what you're good at. He knows your talents. He knows your desires. Why? Because He placed those within you. God wants you to use those gifts to make Him known to other people. If you are walking with Him, pay attention to the God-given desires inside you. Listen to the *compelling.* As Psalm 37:4–6 says, "Delight yourself in the LORD and he will give you the desires of your heart. Commit your way to the LORD; trust in him and he will do this: He will make your righteousness shine like the dawn, the justice of your cause like the noonday sun."

God is so creative. I believe He gives each of us different passions so we can reflect His glory in many different ways. One of my friends, Jeni, is using her passion to develop a part-time business. Whenever Jeni walks into a room, the atmosphere changes. She is a rare individual who has a knack for making everyone she meets feel encouraged, loved, and included. It's hard to find this 30-year-old without a smile on her face.

Three years ago, a group of friends got together and bought Jeni her first karaoke machine. She loved it and began organizing karaoke parties. It didn't take long for the word about Jeni, who is naturally the life of most parties, to spread. People at work asked to borrow the machine and began inviting her to the events to spin discs.

Today, Jeni is the founder of Jeni-oke, a hobby that has grown into a small business. She offers her services as a KJ, the karaoke version of a DJ, and has tons of CDs she can bring to any occasion. She travels to various homes, events, and parties, providing good, clean fun to hundreds of people each year.

Or take Robyn, who began decorating cookies when she was a teenager. As a member of the cheerleading team in high school, she baked cookies for the players before each game. Instead of just buying a tube of cookie dough as I would, Robyn made the cookies from scratch and then cut them into shapes like basketballs and footballs and decorated them with icing. Everyone loved her cookies and asked her to make some for other occasions.

In the meantime, she started decorating birthday cakes for family members. The summer after Robyn graduated she received her first cake order—a twenty-fifth anniversary cake for her friend's parents.

Robyn attended Southern Nazarene University in Bethany, Oklahoma, and graduated with a degree in marketing. She moved back to her hometown of Berryville, Arkansas, and took a job at a local flower shop, but she continued to bake in her spare time. Orders for her baked goods continued coming in. Robyn, with the support of her husband, Josh, eventually made the decision to leave the flower shop and focus on baking full-time. In 2003, the 25-year-old, along with her sister, launched You Take the Cake and Cookies Too!, a bakery specializing in custom-decorated cakes and hand-iced sugar cookies.

"Baking and decorating cakes and cookies is a gift I know God gave me, and I really feel it's the right thing for me to do," Robyn says. "As far as it being a leap or a huge test of faith, I am surrounded by supportive family and friends and customers, and I know that if it is truly God's will then it will work." Before launching the business, Robyn began saving as much money as she could, and decided to have the bakery in her home, which was once owned by her grandmother and where she first learned to make cookies. In addition to supportive family and friends, Robyn says her husband has been incredibly encouraging. "He loves what I do!" she says. "I always wondered who God had out there for me and really wondered if there was such a man who could love and support my creative spirit and not just think I am a crazy creative nut. I am very blessed to have him. He says he's just waiting for my first million so he can quit his job and I can buy him a Harley motorcycle to deliver my cakes on!"

God has an amazing way of using the
desires of our heart to glorify Him.

The compelling God gives you can be, and probably will be, exceptionally different from what He gives to people around you. God has an amazing way of using the desires of our heart to glorify Him. This truth is wonderfully illustrated in the life of one of my personal heroes: Wilson Bentley. A farmer's son, Wilson Bentley grew up in Jericho, Vermont. On his fifteenth birthday, Bentley was given a present that would change his life: a microscope. The naturally inquisitive young man began putting everything he could find, from leaves to flowers to dirt, underneath the lens to see what he could find. The device opened up a whole new world to him.

When the first winter storm hit Jericho, Bentley captured a snowflake and, for the first time, was given a closeup view of the icy creation. He was astounded by the delicate beauty and craftsmanship of the design. He caught another and another and finally ran inside the house to grab a pencil and some paper so he could record each of the unique designs. However, before he could complete any of the drawings, the snowflakes would melt. He noted that whenever a snowflake melted, its design was lost forever. Bentley became determined to preserve the design of snowflakes, and the determination grew into a passion that encompassed his life.

Two years later Bentley was given his first camera, and during the next two years, he developed his own process for photographing snowflakes. On January 15, 1885, Wilson Bentley took the first successful photomicrograph of a snowflake. He was only 19.

Over the next thirteen years, Bentley carefully preserved photomicrographs of more than four hundred snowflakes. He realized the need to share his findings with others and made the trek to a nearby town to share his photographs with a professor.

The images caught the instructor's eye and paved the way for Bentley to publish his first article, "A Study of Snow Crystals," in Appleton's *Popular Science* magazine. Throughout his lifetime, Bentley discovered facts about snowflakes that other scientists in his day failed to notice. He observed that snowflakes typically have six sides, but on rare occasions during dry, cold weather, perfect three-sided snowflakes will form.

Bentley's compelling to understand everything he could about nature caused him to study not just snowflakes but auroras (northern lights) as well. He carefully recorded the auroras he saw from his farmhouse for several years. His work at the turn of the century proved to be so valuable, a presentation at the American Geophysics Union shared his findings nearly eight decades later.

Before he died, this Christian farmer had become known as the foremost authority in the world on snowflakes. His articles appeared in the *New York Times Magazine, National Geographic,* and *Harper's* magazine. Though he photographed more than five thousand snowflakes, he never sold any of them for much more than it cost him to print them. Fortune or fame never compelled Bentley. He was driven by a simple desire to make God's beauty—as displayed in a simple snowflake—known to everyone. Wilson Bentley often made a spiritual connection with what he saw in nature. He observed, "Each snowflake is as different from its fellow as we human beings are from fellows. But the comparison changes there. For each snowflake, if allowed freedom to develop alone, is perfect according to its individual plan. It is one of nature's miracles."[1]

God's calling on each of our lives is unique. No one has the exact same calling, purpose, or mission to fulfill. Pursuing the passion God has for each of us requires that we don't compare ourselves to fellow believers, but set our eyes on our Creator for all He desires to do in and through us as individuals.

Wilson Bentley coined the phrase "No two snowflakes are alike" from his observations. And the same can be said about the calling God has on our lives. The God-given, burning passions we have in our lives—whether to build a house, create art, reach a specific people group or demographic, or even study snowflakes—are meant to be used to glorify God. Bentley once said, "I am a poor man except for the satisfaction I get out of my work. In that respect, I am one of the richest men in the world."[2]

Listen to the nudges of the Holy Spirit. You may be called into ministry or to work with the poor or to start a new business. Follow this compelling. It might upset some people, but remember, different types of stability exist beyond financial stability. Pray, talk to others who have done the same thing, and step out in faith. God knows what He is doing.

He Will Bring It to Pass

Sometimes we have passions within us that lie dormant for a season or two. You may have something you really want to do, something you feel is absolutely from God—whether it be a gift, talent, ministry, idea, or vision—but you find yourself waiting for years, wondering if it will ever happen. I encourage you to continue trusting Him and believe He will bring it to pass.

In *The God Who Hung on the Cross,* Dois Rosser Jr. tells the story of a church being built on swampland in Ukraine after the fall of the Soviet Union. After many years of government control, a new church building was permitted in the region. The Christians in the area filled the entire bog with soil, one wheelbarrow at a time. But by the time the land was prepared for construction, they couldn't get any bricks to build a building.

The government officials allowed them to tear down an old, empty nuclear missile silo nearby left over from the Cold War. As they were taking apart the silo, one man found a brittle piece of paper rolled tightly in between the bricks.

It read, "These bricks were purchased to build a house of worship. But they were confiscated by the government to build a missile silo. May it please the Lord that these bricks will one day be used to build a house to His glory!"[3] Those reading the note realized they were fulfilling this man's written prayer. If God can work things out for a pile of bricks in Russia, imagine what He can do with the gifts and talents He's given you. Never doubt God's faithfulness. He who has begun a good work in you is faithful to complete it.

WHERE DO I GO FROM HERE?

If I could draw a precise road map for every person's life, I would be more successful than Rand McNally. Unfortunately, life isn't as obvious as geometry, and getting from one point to another isn't always as easy as a straight line. Options, opportunities, and decisions line the path, creating turns, curves, and some rather bumpy rides. Every so often I find myself wondering what's around the next corner. Hindsight and some well-developed scrapbooking skills tell me where I've been, but sometimes I hit a roadblock in life that makes me wonder, *Where do I go from here?*

Have you ever experienced one of those moments in life? You know you have to do something—because of either a circumstance or a compelling—but you don't know where to go. During the summer of 2000, I hit one of those crossroads. I was living in a condominium in Melbourne Beach, Florida, and the owners suddenly decided to sell. Without a lease, I knew I had to move. I also knew I didn't have any real attachments to the beachside community and I could move anywhere. I began to pray. I asked God for direction. Where should I live? I prayed harder. No answer. Nothing at all. I remember looking at a map of the United States with its countless possibilities and thinking, *God, just tell me where to go.* I thought about throwing a dart, but I didn't want to put a hole in the freshly painted walls. So I thought, *If I could live anywhere in the entire country, where would I want to live?* One answer came immediately to mind: Colorado. I missed the mountains, my hometown friends, and the outdoors. I prayed about which city to move to, and again, I didn't have any clear direction, so I decided on Colorado Springs. It sounded great, and I knew it had a lot of ministries and solid churches. I called the only person I knew in the area, and he gave me the name of a gal who needed a roommate. I packed my car until I could barely see out the back window and headed west.

With the exception of a few circumstances that seemed to line up, there weren't many clues that I had made the right decision. I didn't drive by any billboards or see any neon lights blaring, "You're on the right path!" But looking back, I realize it was probably the best move I could have made, and just because God didn't make it clear to me doesn't mean He wasn't involved all along.

Finding direction when you're not sure where to go or when you think you've lost your way isn't easy. Fortunately, we don't have to do this thing called life alone. We have a God who knows us, including all the possibilities and the best decisions we can make. If we turn to Him and trust Him, He'll provide the direction we need. Seek God. Pray. Spend time reflecting on the Scriptures. Remember that God cares for His people like a shepherd. In fact, God is referred to as a shepherd in Genesis 48:15, and Jesus describes Himself as "the good shepherd" in John 10:11. Psalm 48:14 promises, "For this God is our God for ever and ever; he will be our guide even to the end."

Just like a shepherd leading sheep, God tends to lead us on a need-to-know basis. Often it isn't connect-the-dots guidance but a general instruction to go where He is going. None of the men or women of the Bible was given a clear road map to follow. They may have had prophetic words uttered over them that gave them a peek into the future, but that's all it was—a peek. In Genesis 12:1, Abraham (known simply as Abram at the time) is instructed by God to "Leave your country, your people and your father's household and go to the land I will show you." He obediently packed up his family and his possessions and set out to follow God. Along the way, God not only appeared to Abraham, He protected him and provided for him. And along our journeys, even when we don't know exactly where we're heading, God will do the same for us.

If you find yourself at one of life's crossroads and have to make a decision, take as much time as possible to wait on God. Talk to counselors, family, and friends who love you and have your best interests in mind. Often God will speak through those who know you best. Sometimes, though, we have to make a decision without clear-cut guidance. In those times, pray and ask God to go before you. Ask God that His will is done. It's in these decision times that we're given a greater opportunity to know and trust the One who directs all things.

And remember that despite the pressure you feel, the entire universe isn't hanging in the balance based on your decision. Growing up, by nature, requires that you move forward. You must make decisions, and inherently a decision forces you to say no to one thing so you can say yes to something else.

Josh, a 29-year-old graduate of the University of California, Santa Cruz, says that by far the biggest lesson he has learned in his twenties is that God is far more concerned with who you're becoming than what road you're on to get there. "He is more concerned with my heart and not so much with what school I choose, what church I attend, or what career path I decide to take," Josh says. "Throughout my twenties, I stressed out so much regarding whether or not I was in the Lord's will and if I was hearing the Lord's voice." Josh says he can remember sitting on the floor of his summer "shack," trying to hear from the Lord regarding a decision he had to make between two schools. "I put both catalogs side by side on the floor and asked God to levitate the one He wanted me to go to," Josh says lightheartedly. "But nothing happened. I was so afraid of being outside the will of God, and I really missed the whole point of God's will. When you're in your twenties, the tendency is to become obsessed with issues of God's will in regard to the choices you're making concerning your life's direction and forget that God is more concerned with your heart and the type of person you are becoming."

The good news is, as Josh and others attest, even when you don't know what is next in your life, God does. He isn't nervous. He isn't freaking out. He isn't sitting on the edge of His throne, wondering if you'll be able to make it through okay. So even when you feel that you've lost the road map to life, no worries. He has it all under control.

FAST FACTS

→ Marrying Later: According to the U.S. Census Bureau, since our parents' generation, the median age of marriage for men has risen from 22 to 27, and the median age of women has risen from 20 to 24. ("Insurance Gets Hip," *American Demographics,* January 1, 2002, 48.)

→ Losing Religion: When surveyed, 89 percent of twenty-somethings said they believed in God, but only 48 percent attend church services. ("Millennial Morals," *American Demographics,* August 1, 2001.)

the questions that
connect us to others

One of the most humbling realizations for my independent personality has been the realization that I need other people. I am no island. I need healthy relationships around me to keep me balanced, to keep me accountable, and to keep me connected.

Muhammad Ali, the famed world-boxing champion, was known for both his wit and sense of humor. But one lighthearted story tells of the boxer being outdone by another. Reportedly, he was on a plane that had hit some turbulence. The flight attendant immediately ordered that everyone on board fasten their seat belts. Everyone complied except Muhammad Ali. When the flight attendant went over to the boxer and asked him to put on his seat belt, he looked at her and said, "Superman don't need no seat belt."

Without a pause, she responded, "Superman don't need no airplane either!"[1]

Like Ali, a lot of twentysomethings are a little cocky about their flight out of the family nest. After being set up by two, four, or even more years of college, it's easy to become a little overly self-confident. But you eventually discover you can't do it alone. You need people around you for accountability, comfort, companionship, and everything else that is provided by real relationships.

WHY DO I FEEL ALONE SOMETIMES?

I'm no George Barna, but I have informally surveyed dozens of twentysomethings around the country and asked about the biggest challenges of being in your twenties. While finances and relationships topped the list, loneliness resonated among a surprising number of those who responded. Interestingly, loneliness was cited more often among young married people than singles.

One person, whether it's your spouse or best friend, cannot meet all your relational needs. You are designed to have a fabric of solid, healthy friendships around you, but weaving a rich tapestry of friends isn't always easy.

Laura, a 30-year-old who has been married for the last seven years, said that after college it got a lot harder for her to make friends. She decided to attend law school and thought it would provide a forum for building new relationships. "After three years in school, I never met anyone who will be much more than a close acquaintance," she recalls. "The irony is, the larger the city, the harder I found it to develop real relationships. I thought living in a big city meant more people and, therefore, better chances of meeting people you would really bond with. As it turns out, coming to a small town was the best thing I could have done. In a year and a half, in a county with a total population of about sixty thousand, where only half the population finished high school and the economy flat-lined years ago, I have made more friends and social acquaintances than I did from 21 to 27. What is really funny is that my friends here are more nationally diverse than any I have ever had."

Twentysomethings are highly relational. We know we need each other. This world is too challenging to go at it alone. God instills the desire for friends and healthy relationships in us. Clinical psychologist and counselor John Townsend says we were designed by God to need each other. He believes dependence and need are not negative. Relationships are not luxuries—they are *necessities.*

Relationships give you the ability to feel loved inside. When people talk negatively about themselves, well-meaning friends may say, "You just need to like yourself more." Townsend says knowing you are loved has to come from reaching out to other people. When you realize others care about you deeply and want to connect with you, it's much easier to give yourself a little slack when your imperfections can't be ignored.

Healthy relationships with others provide encouragement when you are discouraged. Friends provide comfort when you're hurting and compassion when you're struggling. They provide hope when you fail. These kinds of relationships remind us of a powerful little word: *grace.* The Bible defines *grace* as undeserved favor. Grace is the reality that God is on your side. Friends are the evidence of that fact. You are not alone. Even with all your imperfections, you are valuable and loved.

"You can't function in the twenty-first century without believing that people are on your side," Townsend says. "Without it, you run the risk of caving in, giving up, or even developing emotional issues because life is too hard."[2]

The importance of relationships cannot be understated. Relationships are essential to both your emotional health and your spiritual health. One of the questions I have repeatedly asked pastors of twentysomethings is, "What makes the difference between a twentysomething who grows in their faith and one who grows stagnant or falls away?" Without fail, relationships and community were most often cited as the determining factors for growth.

"The one thing I have found about this generation is that they are extremely communal," says Mike Sares, pastor of Scum of the Earth Church in Denver, Colorado. "Friends are more important than anything else. With homes broken by divorce and the ties to the nuclear family less strong, developing a community is extremely important in their maturation as Christians."

A Longing for Community

Whenever you feel lonely, remember that loneliness can be a motivating force that causes us to reach out to others rather than withdraw from them. We all need points of connection with others. A strong community can be hard to find. If you have one, count yourself blessed. If you don't have one, you need to be proactive about looking for a community or building one. Sometimes community can be found in a small group, singles group, young married group, or Bible study. You may find that sense of community among coworkers or in a sports league. The important thing is to find people who will affirm, love, and care for you. You need people who know you—your strengths and weaknesses—and can lovingly challenge you.

Joy, a 23-year-old development coordinator for Vanderbilt University Medical Center, wondered if a move to a small city would be the answer. After growing up in Auburn, Alabama, and graduating from Auburn University, she took a job in a larger city where she struggled to make friends and find a community. Describing the transition, she says, "I hated being gone to work all day long, then being exhausted at the end of the day. I didn't have many friends right at the beginning, and it's hard to get motivated to make friends and to create that fun and diversion you desperately need. Life gets monotonous pretty quick if you aren't proactive."

Joy eventually found a church she liked and decided to join. "That has probably been the greatest thing and made more difference than anything else," she says. "I feel at home, I'm busy with events and friends, and I truly enjoy where I am in life."

Almost everyone says they want community, but most are unaware of the high price. True community isn't just a group of friends. It's gut-level sharing, caring, and going through life together. It's praying for each other. It means being there for each other even when it's not convenient. It means confronting sin, holding each other accountable, and fully exposing your shortcomings, all the while encouraging each other spiritually.

I've experienced a "honeymoon period" with almost every group of people I've chosen to hang out with. Whether it's fellow employees, a small group at a church, or a tribe of friends, I find myself going into the group thinking everyone is wonderful and gets along great. It usually doesn't take long before I begin to pick up on conflicts between personalities, annoying habits, and unresolved tensions. It's at that point—when I am forced to confront my own weaknesses and sins and have the choice to accept or reject those of the other people—the value of true community emerges. People like to throw around the term *community* a lot as a refuge and support network. And it is that, but true community means more—much more. Community forces us to confront the nitty-gritty of our selfishness, pride, and judgmental attitudes. It forces us to seek grace, to forgive, to repent, and to learn how to love unconditionally.

Rachel, a 25-year-old coordinator for the Kairos Community in Washington, D.C., observes, "God calls us to community so we can see a mirror and reflection of ourselves. And if you stay in a community long enough—without moving or trading the group in for a better one—you'll experience the richness of the real relationships God intended."[3]

As a side note, while no community of people is perfect, some communities are downright unhealthy. One way to evaluate the strength of your community is to evaluate how the people treat you when you're down. Do they ignore you? Do they act disappointed in you? Do they tell you to try harder or suggest you have a personal sin in your life? If so, the community may not be providing enough support. It is always difficult to start fresh, but you may want to look for a new community that will celebrate with your joys, mourn with your losses, and help you stand when you need encouragement.

WILL ANYONE EVER LOVE ME?

I have known many people throughout my life—both men and women—who have always wanted to be married. I have female friends who can describe the details of their dream wedding dress and name their bridesmaids in alphabetical order by either first or last name. They can tell you the time of day and season of the year they want to be married, as well as the approximate number of guests that will be attending the event. They can do all this—even when there isn't a prospective partner in sight.

I never really cared. I didn't even have a real desire to be married until late into my twenties. For whatever reason, I rarely went to bed with the sound of wedding bells dancing in my head. When I graduated from college single, I knew I was being given an opportunity to make the most of my single years. And I did. I averaged about one move per year for the first six years out of college. I took road trips across the country to visit old friends. I attended Bible college. I spent two summers in Alaska working at my aunt's bed-and-breakfast. I learned how to find travel bargains on the Internet and used my single status as a badge of freedom to travel at the drop of a hat or at least the drop in an airline ticket price. I trained for a marathon and hiked 14ers (mountains over fourteen thousand feet tall). I worked as a ski instructor and kids' adventure camp counselor. Since I was a child, I've had a list of things I wanted to do during my lifetime, and I used my unmarried years to accomplish them. From visiting Hawaii to publishing my first book, I started crossing the accomplishments off my mental list. I had read that the average age of a person getting married these days is 26 (four years later than it was in 1970), so I wasn't too worried about meeting someone soon.[4]

Everything was going along smoothly until somewhere around my twenty-seventh birthday. My birthday is in March, during the onset of spring, when everything is in bloom and love is in the air. I had passed through previous springs unscathed, but this one caught me off guard. Maybe it was my grandmother's birthday wishes, which included a comment about "being an old maid." Maybe it was the realization that the big "three-oh" was rapidly approaching. Maybe it was the sense that everything was in bloom but me. Or maybe it was the fact that I was nearing the end of my lifelong to-do list and needed fresh additions like visiting the Mall of America or convincing the cast of *While You Were Out* to redo a room in my home. I'm still not sure, but I remember waking up one morning and thinking, *I really want to be married.*

I tried to make the thought go away. Really, I did. But it didn't budge. The worst part was that the thought didn't go away by the end of the day or even the next month. As much as I threw myself into work, purchased more bargain airline tickets on Priceline.com, or attended social events with my great group of friends, I knew I wanted to settle down with someone. What had been happening to everyone else for years was finally happening to me, and I didn't like it one bit.

Oddly, I noticed my desire for a companion intensified when life was at its best. Long hikes in the woods, breathtaking sunsets, and snuggly warm blankets on a cold winter's day made me long to share my life with someone. I could pass through the lonely moments or bad days without a second thought of that someone special, but when life was really grand, I desperately wanted to share it with someone.

One of my greatest passions—traveling—began to lose its luster. Years ago, I watched an interview with Lionel Richie on *Oprah*. He made the sagelike observation that when you travel, you should always take the people you love most with you, because when you return you're never the same person. I never forgot those words. I was taking all kinds of amazing trips with friends, but deep in my soul I wanted to travel in the company of someone with whom I could share the memories for a lifetime.

My desire to travel solo began to diminish. I remember the time I took an amazing ocean-discovery tour in Alaska. Otters frolicked in groups along the lines of seaweed, killer whales broke the surface of the icy waters in large groups, and puffins nested beside each other along the rocky shore. I went belowdecks to warm myself and took a seat along with the hundred or so tourists on board. Couples sat in warm embraces. Parents held their children. Families nestled close together. I was alone. And I felt alone.

This was one of those incredible moments in life—experiencing the Alaskan shoreline—and I had no one to share it with. From that time on, I also began to experience a social awkwardness that developed as a result of my singleness. I would be caught off guard in situations that I would later learn to avoid completely. I remember attending a wedding at the top of Vail Ski Resort in Colorado. It was a glorious affair, complete with spectacular views and fine food. I was not dating anyone at the time. When I asked to bring along a friend as a date, I was told seating was limited and no additional guests were allowed, so I decided to attend the wedding on my own. I knew only a handful of people at the event, and I had no one to hide behind. No one I could latch onto for security when insecurity began to ooze from the innermost parts of my being. I felt as if everyone else in the room noticed that I was single. A fumbled attempt to introduce me to someone by a well-meaning friend highlighted my perception, even if it wasn't true. I felt like a poster child for social awkwardness.

During the appetizers, I couldn't bear the sting in my soul any longer, and I headed to the bathroom for a good cry. I thought it

would help, but it only opened up a floodgate of pain and insecurities that had been lying beneath the surface of my happy-go-
lucky singleness for years. I left the event early and promised myself
I would never attend another wedding solo again and would avoid
all other potential *Bridget Jones's Diary* moments at all costs.

The truth is that being single can be brutal. No matter how
much you love God. No matter how much you trust Him. No matter how much you come to terms with your singleness and make
the most of the years. Hard days still exist.

The worst part about the desire to be married was that it wasn't
just intensifying in me; it was also beginning to affect all my other
late-twenties single friends. We had all seen the wedding seasons
come and go. You know, those seasons when it seems everyone you
know is getting married, except for you. Wedding seasons hit work-
places, singles groups, and informal gatherings of friends. One day
no one is dating, and the next day it seems everyone is tying the
knot. My friends and I had survived several wedding seasons and
the baby seasons that follow. We were growing tired of throwing
showers for everyone else and ready to enjoy the experience of these
events for ourselves.

Waiting for "the One"

All the pat answers we had been given by pastors, well-meaning
Christian friends, and those countless dating/singles books were
wearing thin. My friends and I—both male and female—had gone
through the stages of "kissing dating good-bye," only to discover
you had to "kiss dating hello" every so often or you'd never leave the
house. We had become content with our singleness, even celebrat-
ing it. We had used the years to pursue God, build healthy relation-

ships, and develop as individuals. We had circled through the stages of brokenness, discontentment, and contentment enough times to get dizzy. We had patiently waited. We had persistently prayed. We had given our hearts to God so many times, we secretly wondered if there was anything left to give to "the one" . . . if the person ever came around at all.

And we wondered, *Where is "the one"?* Did the knight in shining armor lose the trail map? Had he fed the horse some bad hay? Was he backslidden from God? Please, God, tell me he isn't the dorky neighbor living three doors down the street, whom I really don't want to marry.

Lori Smith, author of *The Single Truth: Challenging the Misconceptions of Singleness with God's Consuming Truth,* says she has asked herself many of the same questions. She said friends have tried to comfort her with hollow offerings of encouragement. The top three include

1. When you're ready or content or not looking, the person will arrive.

2. The Lord must still be working on that special someone.

3. God has the perfect person, so just be patient.

"I was angered by the simple way people dealt with the issue of my singleness and then moved on," she says. "It was like people were saying, 'I'm not going to accept your singleness or deal with it.' They saw it as a temporary problem with a long-term solution around the corner. They also made the assumption that if God worked one way in their life then He would work the same way in my life."

Lori says she grew increasingly discontented with her single status until a friend finally challenged her with the question, "What do you want your life to be if you never get married?" The question stung. Lori wrestled over it for some time before coming to terms with the fact that she may never marry and that God had a plan for her as a single person. Lori did an in-depth study in the life of Jeremiah. She studied the popular verse that says, "'For I know the plans I have for you,' declares the LORD, 'plans to prosper you and not to harm you, plans to give you hope and a future'" (Jeremiah 29:11). She says the verse is often used to remind believers that God has great plans for their lives, but if you look at the context of when God spoke this word, Jeremiah was in a difficult spot. He was being called to declare challenging words to God's people.

God had good plans for Jeremiah, but they weren't the everything-works-out-just-as-you-like-it kind of plans. "That verse is much more about God's overall sovereignty and His ultimate plan," Lori says. "It's not so much about the details, like you're going to have a husband or raise children or live in a certain house."

Lori says she's in a place now where it would be difficult to give up all her single freedoms if marriage did come her way. "I still want to be married someday, but I think I'm taking advantage of all the good things about being single, and realizing that when marriage becomes a possibility, I'll be trading in one set of blessings for another, not necessarily trading up."[5]

Waiting for the one isn't easy, but neither is marriage.

After Tying the Knot

Of course, after you find *the one*, plan the wedding, and go on a honeymoon, life gets even more complicated. Marriage isn't a piece of cake—at least not like the one you served at your wedding. You can expect ups and downs. Everyone says marriage is work, and both people have to give 100 percent (if not more) to make it work. Yet no one can tell you what marriage is really like. No matter how many late-night, let's-get-real conversations with married friends, it's impossible to know all the realities of marriage until you've tied the knot.

Cari Stone, in her poignant article "Forgoing Dink Status," writes,

Not long into our marriage—maybe a month—my husband became intimately acquainted with a new side of my demeanor. How his usually happy, even-keeled friend could disintegrate into a sobbing mess in under a minute to this day puzzles him. But back then, such meltdowns were beyond reason—especially considering that the culprit in this particular case was not a horrible argument, but simply a pile of dirty clothes. It wasn't about the dirty clothes. Sure, maybe that stack of boxers pushed me over the edge, but ultimately the tears flowed far beyond this mess.

Stone writes that she was a new wife pulled in all directions. Her job was demanding and her evening hours were spent attempting to cook something other than Easy Mac while simultaneously trying to figure out how to relate to her new lifelong roommate.

"He's a great guy and frankly as low-maintenance as they come," she said. "Nonetheless, simply interacting at this new level of husband and wife took time and energy. So did setting up a house, paying bills, grocery shopping for two, scheduling social activities . . . and doing laundry. That night I succumbed to the pressure somewhere between burning chicken and relearning how to fold T-shirts according to the male model."[6]

Cari is one of the few women who are honest enough to admit the transition from single life to married life isn't easy. At times it's wonderful, thrilling, and compelling. And at other times, it's enough to put you (or him) on the path to a mini mental breakdown.

Marriage is lots of hard work. It's lots of compromise. And it isn't always a cure for being alone. There will be times he (or she) won't be with you. My friends Kelly and Lauri discovered this when a few short months after their weddings, they were invited to attend a mutual friend's wedding. Due to work commitments, neither of their husbands could attend. Though they were married, both women were attending a wedding by themselves, along with all the unmarried women. Single people tend to make a lot of assumptions about what married life will be like. But just because you're married doesn't mean you will have a date every Friday night. He or she may have to work or be too tired. Just because you're married doesn't mean you don't have to maintain a healthy network of loving friends and support. Your spouse can't be everything to you. And just because you're married doesn't mean that loneliness won't still strike from time to time.

Most of us have single friends who want to be married and some married friends who may miss some of the aspects of a single life. The secret to a successful life is being content, regardless of your marital status. Of course, some days that is easier than others, and it's always easier to say it than to live it.

WHY IS NO ONE CLAPPING?

Do you have a box somewhere filled with the relics of your accomplishments from childhood? Maybe it's in your parents' attic. Maybe it's in one of your closets. Or maybe it's packed away in a storage unit somewhere.

What's in your box?

Most people's boxes contain an assortment of memorabilia such as a ribbon from a field day, a graduation certificate from kindergarten, a trophy for a sports event, or a plaque recognizing an accomplishment. It seemed that almost every event in school—from a spelling bee to a debate tournament to a swim meet—ended in an awards ceremony. Depending on your level of involvement with school activities, you may have a stack of ribbons, certificates, and trophies packed away.

If you ever go back and look inside your own box of memorabilia, you'll find that behind every award was an affirmation. You were being applauded. You were being recognized. You were being celebrated. *Good job. Well done! You did great! I'm proud of you.* That's one reason it's hard to get rid of the box. The other reason, of course, is that your mom told you never to throw them away.

But once you step out of the school system, awards and pats on the back are a lot more difficult to come by. You may be told that you're a great worker during your annual job review. You may get a raise. You may get a promotion. You may get an article written about you in a newspaper or magazine. But unless you're joining every sporting league in town—from bowling to volleyball to soccer—those ribbons, certificates, and trophies are a lot harder to come by.

The lack of affirmation in adulthood can be particularly difficult for anyone who was recognized during school as possessing a unique talent, skill, or ability. You may have been an incredible vocalist, instrumentalist, or basketball player in high school, but now, in your twenties, you don't get to use or showcase your gift. When that rare opportunity arises, you may not stand out as you used to. Your talent or skill may be dismissed as commonplace, especially if you're in a field where many people share the same talent. The affirmation you have been receiving for years has stopped, leaving you to quietly wonder, *Why is no one clapping?*

The Need for Affirmation

Somewhere in the soul of every human being is the need for affirmation. You need it. I need it. We all need it. When we don't get it, something just seems wrong. We think we have to try harder, perform better, become more attractive, or attain more—just to get that seal of approval. Whether you're a little kid or a big kid, we all have a natural tendency to go where we are affirmed.

Let me ask you, where do you go to get your affirmation?

While we may desire ribbons and certificates or promotions and raises to remind us that we are affirmed, true affirmation—the kind that satisfies the hunger of the soul—comes only from God.

God often will use the people around you to affirm you. John Townsend, coauthor of *How People Grow,* says that we tend not to see ourselves as we really are. "Nobody has a perfectly clear self-image," he says. "It's affected by past experiences and misinterpretations. When we undergo these sorts of hurtful self-condemnations, affirmation helps clarify the reality that even though we aren't perfect, we are not all bad either, and that we are loved and valued by those who know us."[7]

Affirmation is crucial when you are going to take a risk— whether it's a new job, a big move, or stepping out in a new direction. Everyone needs cheerleaders, and God often will place people around you to encourage and challenge you. Walking in the affirmation of God is crucial. This truth was demonstrated during the baptism of Jesus. Mark 1:10 says, "As Jesus was coming up out of the water, he saw heaven being torn open and the Spirit descending on him like a dove."

Can you imagine seeing heaven torn open? Or watching the Spirit descend on you? This passage describes an incredibly powerful moment, but even more powerful are the words that follow. Mark 1:11 says, "And a voice came from heaven: 'You are my Son, whom I love; with you I am well pleased.'" God's voice echoed through the heavens. Jesus and all those around Him heard the powerful words of affirmation. God affirmed Jesus as His Son, God affirmed Jesus in His love, and God affirmed Jesus as One in whom He was well pleased.

In *Jesus Driven Ministry,* Ajith Fernando observes, "First, by calling Jesus his beloved Son, God satisfied the human need for identity. Second, by saying that he is pleased with Jesus, God satisfied the need for security. If God is pleased with us, there is nothing to fear. Paul said, 'If God is for us, who can be against us?' (Romans 8:31). Third, by affirming that Jesus is the Messiah, God satisfied the human need for significance. Jesus had an important work to do."[8]

Did you notice where this affirmation came in Jesus' ministry? It came at the very beginning. Before Jesus worked a single miracle, before He made a single convert, and before He battled the decision in the Garden of Gethsemane to embrace the Cross, Jesus was already fully affirmed by the Father. Did Jesus need the affirmation? I don't know. But I do know that you and I need the affirmation, not just when we're feeling a little down, but every day.

FINDING GOD'S AFFIRMATION

→ Know what the Bible says about you.

→ Spend time in prayer and worship.

→ Recognize that God will use other people to affirm you in His love.

→ Remember whose you are.

Walking in the Affirmation

When you live in the affirmation of God, you can't help but live differently. You live with God's smile on your life. You feel His presence. You are filled with the peace that breeds joy even on difficult days. When you walk in the affirmation of God, you are free from having to seek excessive encouragement from other people. You don't have to hope that someone, somewhere, will validate you. You are free to be who God created you to be. You are less likely to compromise, grow discouraged, or react negatively to situations. You no longer have to live up to other people's expectations or seek worldly applause, because you have the encouragement from the One who really matters.

When you are affirmed by God, you can affirm others. You can encourage them in their own gifts and talents because you are secure in your own. You can challenge those around you to become who God has called them to be. You can nurture others. Your relationships become healthier because the roots of competition, greed, or control have been removed. You can be a more effective servant and become a more graceful leader.

When God affirms you, you can be honest with yourself about

your shortcomings. You can remember that God's strength truly is perfected in our weaknesses.

How do you walk in affirmation? First, you need to know what the Bible says about you. Many of the Scriptures that speak of your identity in Christ speak also of your affirmation in Him. God's love for you is consistent. He loves you just as much when you have a bad hair day as when you have a good one. In other words, God's love toward you is not based on you. It's based on Him—His faithfulness, His goodness, and His everlasting kindness. In addition, spending time in prayer and worship can make a huge difference. When you spend time worshiping God for who He is, you take your eyes off yourself and focus on God. In the process, your perception changes. You begin to see things as God sees them—and you begin to see yourself as God sees you.

It's also important to keep an eye out for others God will use to affirm you. Some people are better at letting God affirm them, and some people are better at letting God use people to affirm them. You need both. Every time I receive a note—whether it's an e-mail, letter, or card—that is particularly encouraging, I place it in a file in my desk drawer. Every so often, when I'm having a bad day, I will pull out the file and remember all the people God has placed in my life who love and support me. I read stories of how God used me, even when I didn't know it, to encourage someone else, and I'm reminded of the fingerprints of God all over my life. I see His affirmation through the eyes of others.

Finally, always remember whose you are. God designed you perfectly, which you may forget some days, but that doesn't mean it's not true. God fashioned you in His image, and He loves what He sees. You may be able to point out your flaws or blemishes—but He designed and created you just that way for a reason. When you need affirmation, run to the One who created you and ask Him what He thinks of you. You won't be disappointed.

WHAT IS REAL?

The color of the postmodern world is gray. The world today would have us believe there's nothing such as truth or certainty. Ravi Zacharias illustrates this point by recalling a time he was lecturing at Ohio State University, one of the largest universities in the country. Minutes away from beginning his speech, his host was driving past a new building called the Wexner Center for Performing Arts.

The host observed, "This is America's first postmodern building."

Unfamiliar with this form of architecture, Zacharias asked him to explain.

He replied, "The architect said that he designed this building with no design in mind. When the architect was asked, 'Why?' he said, 'If life itself is capricious, why should our buildings have any design and any meaning?' So he has pillars that have no purpose. He has stairways that go nowhere. He had a senseless building built and somebody has paid for it."

Zacharias asked, "So his argument was that if life has no purpose and design, why should the building have any design?"

The host responded, "That is correct."

To which Zacharias pressed, "Did he do the same with the foundation?"

The host was silent.

Zacharias described the moment that followed: "All of a sudden there was silence. You see, you and I can fool with the infrastructure as much as we would like, but we dare not fool with the foundation because it will call our bluff in a hurry."[9]

Despite the fact that we are on the tail end of a postmodern world and on the brink of a new era, the human heart still longs for truth. It desires something solid with meaning and value on which to base its beliefs. *What is real?* In so many ways, we live in a faux world. It seems almost everything real has its cheap imitation— faux leather, faux fur, and faux fashions. You can find hundreds of items, from Gucci bags to Oakley sunglasses, that are just repro- ductions of the real thing. You can buy a knockoff for a fraction of the cost. You know you have a fake, but others can't really tell the difference. Unfortunately, I've met faux Christians. They utter the right spiritual phrases, have their radio on the Christian station whenever you get in their car, and avidly attend a local church, but they don't really believe in Jesus. Harsh, but true.

One man who had been teaching Sunday school at my church for over a month pulled me aside one night and asked if I really believed this "Jesus is the Son of God and He died for your sins kind of thing." We talked for the next few hours. He asked tough questions. "Does that mean if someone in a tribe in Africa never hears about Jesus and dies, then they're going to hell?"; "What's going to happen to all those Muslim people?"; and "Why did my relative, who was a Christian, die from cancer at such a young age?"

In my head, I was thinking, *Uh . . . can I get back to you on that one?* But I managed to share the best biblically based answers I could. Over the course of our conversation, I was able to share why I believed "the whole Jesus thing" and why His sacrifice means so much to me. When the conversation was over, I couldn't help but wonder how a man who wasn't even a Christian slipped into a leadership position at the church and was teaching Sunday school. It wasn't his fault. He wasn't trying to be a faux Christian; he was just trying to learn more about faith in a church that needed workers rather than disciples.

Something about the man's honesty and candor gripped me. No, he wasn't a Christian, but he was being real. He was bold enough to admit he was struggling with the concepts he was teaching. He was grappling with the basic tenets of the faith. He was trying to get to the heart of the matter. He was asking, *What's real?*

If the truth be told, I am, too.

I believe the basics. Jesus. Son of God. Died. Resurrected. Believe. Salvation. Personal relationship. Grow. Stumble. Fall. Grow some more. Become like Jesus. But I want to live out the reality of those basics every day. I don't want a faith that doesn't change me. I want something real, and I want to be around others who want to live out their faith in a real way, too. I long to be around people who are willing to be real and admit they're struggling. I don't want a theological answer or an argument that is shallow or irrelevant; I've decided I'm going to dig until I find the tangible truth. I want to live the *authentic life*.

What Is the Authentic Life?

The authentic life means recognizing that if we aren't careful, we can become part of a subculture that doesn't impact the people or the world around us. If we aren't aware of our tendencies, we may wake up one day and find ourselves completely surrounded by Christians, but failing to engage the world around us. It may feel safe, but it is a false haven for those called to live in a messy world. It is possible to create your own little world that has little to no contact with or impact on the outside world. But living an authentic life requires stepping outside this "holy bubble" and reaching people who are dying without Jesus.

The authentic life requires admitting faults and weaknesses. Despite society's pressure to conform and present yourself as having it all together, an immense power resides in showing your faults and weaknesses you wish no one would see. When you are real about your failings, people connect with you.

My father was never a big fan of preachers, but there was one he always wanted to get to church early to hear—Jamie Buckingham. I asked my father why Jamie was his favorite, and he explained that every Sunday, Jamie would get up and share something from his life where he had really made a mistake. He would tell the congregation about a fight with his wife, a moment when he spoke a four-letter word about another driver, or some other time when he behaved less than his Sunday best. My father could always relate to Jamie, and it made the message of Jesus more real to him. Jamie Buckingham passed away a number of years ago, but from time to time I'll still hear my dad quote something Jamie used to say: "Honesty has longevity."

If you want to live the authentic life, you have to be brutally honest about your imperfections. You can't try to hide them or cover them up. You must become transparent. It is living with a desire to be real, honest, and genuine. Andrew Murray once wrote, "The great poison of our dealing with divine things is superficiality."[10] The authentic life means offering more than stock Sunday school answers or pretending to know it all. It's a willingness to learn. Living the authentic life means asking, "How are you?" and really wanting to hear the answer. It is pushing the level of conversation beyond a review of the last movie you saw, who won the game, and what the weather is like.

The authentic life means identifying with those around you. If you're going to live this type of life and seek to be in real relationship with those around you, you have to be able to identify with others. You have to remove any pedestals, perceived or real, you might have underneath your feet and be honest. You will have to stop running away from intimate relationships and running toward those who will embrace you, failings and all.

John Ruhlman, a pastor at Life Community Church in Temecula Valley, California, was speaking at his church one Sunday out of the eighth chapter of Luke, where the woman reaches out to touch the hem of Jesus' clothing and is healed. He spoke of how many of us rub shoulders with Jesus, but how few have the faith to touch His garment and see if He'll heal us. Rather than invite the congregation up to the altar following the message, Ruhlman says he realized he was the one who needed to go to the front first. "I want to be the first one who is making the commitment," he announced. "Does anyone else want to come with me?" The response was overwhelming.[11]

People crave to be around others who are real and can identify with their needs, not in the "I know what you're going through" kind of way because, honestly, you can't know *exactly* what someone else is going through. But rather in the "I've struggled with that, too, and I'm here to listen if you need me" kind of way.

Finally, *the authentic life means admitting that we can fall into the trap of just "doing" Christianity.* Unless our lives are infused with the life and light of God every day, we can easily trespass into dead religion. I sometimes find myself going through the same spiritual disciplines—reading the Bible and praying in the morning—with little impact or effect. If someone asked me five minutes afterward what I had read, I'd have to admit that I couldn't remember. Those times weren't connecting points with God for me, and if I go through enough days in a row without connecting with God, I find myself feeling miles away from Him, even though I can still fill out my imaginary checklist of Christian disciplines. No one is immune from drifting away in his or her relationship with God. The authentic life and living real Christianity mean being honest with ourselves and others when we're in one of those dry seasons, and nourishing and encouraging each other out of them.

◎   ◎   ◎

Why bother trying to live the authentic life? Because the authentic life makes an impact. Its significance echoes in eternity. Jesus lived the authentic life. When you live the authentic life you begin to enter into real relationships with other people and grow together. And you might be surprised at what you learn in the process.

MATTHEW 6:25–34

Therefore I tell you, do not worry about your life, what you will eat or drink; or about your body, what you will wear. Is not life more important than food, and the body more important than clothes? Look at the birds of the air; they do not sow or reap or store away in barns, and yet your heavenly Father feeds them. Are you not much more valuable than they? Who of you by worrying can add a single hour to his life?

And why do you worry about clothes? See how the lilies of the field grow. They do not labor or spin. Yet I tell you that not even Solomon in all his splendor was dressed like one of these. If that is how God clothes the grass of the field, which is here today and tomorrow is thrown into the fire, will he not much more clothe you, O you of little faith? So do not worry, saying, "What shall we eat?" or "What shall we drink?" or "What shall we wear?" For the pagans run after all these things, and your heavenly Father knows that you need them. But seek first his kingdom and his righteousness, and all these things will be given to you as well. Therefore do not worry about tomorrow, for tomorrow will worry about itself. Each day has enough trouble of its own.

when hard times happen

It's kind of weird. I have never gone out looking for hard times, but they still manage to find me. I've even tried hiding from them by wearing my seat belt, eating lots of green vegetables, and not getting too involved in complex situations. I've tried to protect myself from hard times, but sooner or later they still come knocking on my door. Slowly, I'm coming to terms with the fact that hard times happen. That's a Christian-esque way of saying you-know-what happens. Yet even when it hits the fan, it's not without God knowing. And there's a bit of comfort in that, even though everything smells a little funky.

When I was a freshman in high school, I remember eying this "older" man—a junior—who wasn't really flirting with me but was just trying to be friendly. He drove a Jeep, and if your high school was like mine, a Jeep—or any car with four wheels—always beat riding on the yellow bus with torn vinyl seat covers. One day my emotions finally got the best of me, and on a school trip together, I confessed to him that I loved him. He looked back and said, "That's nice."

Ouch. Not what I wanted to hear . . .

It was one of my first real-life lessons that things don't always turn out as you hope they will. Granted, I'd put this event in the category of low-grade, adolescent hard times, but it still stunk nonetheless. I'd love to say that was pretty much the end of my experience with hard times. Instead, I must say I've been tossed around, beat up, and hung out to dry as life has continued.

These twentysomething years aren't without more than their fair share of hard times. Basic economics, relationships, and spiritual issues all challenge us from time to time. Financially, you may have to make loan payments, climb out of credit card debt, find a job that makes over $19,000 a year, learn how to invest, and then figure out how to live on less than you make. It's not easy. Relationally, you have to develop a strong network of friends and redefine your relationship as an adult with one or both parents, as well as maintain lifelong friendships. On top of all that, there is the issue of figuring out *if* you're supposed to marry and, if so, finding Mr. or Mrs. Right and then maintaining a marriage that is healthy and glorifying to God. On the spiritual side of things, you have to make the adjustment of making your faith your own instead of relying on what others have told you, and discovering how best to keep your relationship with Christ alive and vibrant. So in case you might have missed it: There is a lot going on during your twenties!

But if all this wasn't enough, you also have to handle a frequent visitor: hard times. They take many forms—the loss of a loved one, an illness, an accident—a long list of things we didn't think could happen to us or anyone we know, at least not at our age. When you're in your twenties, it's easy to think *that* kind of stuff happens only to other people.

Not all hard times are dramatic or tragic. The more common hard times are much smaller in their scope and impact. A hope is deferred. A trust is betrayed. A viewpoint is opposed. A decision is challenged. Sometimes hard times take the form of everyday stress. Rebecca, a 24-year-old caseworker for an adoption service in North Carolina, says the sheer weight of the responsibility of her job stresses her out. In college, only her test grades and time management skills affected her. Now, she's finding that in her marriage and in her job, her decisions have a much greater significance than before. "This stress has been hard to deal with," she says. "In college, it was easy to just call a friend with problems, but now, with my best friends all over the country and with the issues at hand being much more serious, I feel that God is the only One who can truly carry the burden of my anxiety and fear about the real world."

Rebecca isn't the only one encountering stress and anxiety. Winn, a 31-year-old college pastor, says he had a breakdown of sorts while in seminary. Looking back, he says he was too busy with seventeen hours a semester of graduate school work and driving about six hundred miles a week between his ministry, job, and school. At the time, he was also working another part-time marketing job on the side to help pay school bills.

"On top of that, I was struggling to figure out who I was and facing some serious spiritual issues in my life, was in a long-distance relationship with Miska (who is now my wife), and felt incredibly lonely," he says. "I slumped into some sort of depression for a couple of months. All I could do was sleep, and I lost a good bit of weight—

the weird thing was that few people noticed. Anyway, through some time, a counselor, and more time, the depression eased up."

After seminary, Winn says he began working for a pastor for whom he eventually lost all respect. Through two years of incredible struggle, he realized that both his integrity and health required that he and his wife leave. "So, we did—but not before the pastor berated me, telling me I was absolutely useless and had been an utter failure there," he says. "Those words and that experience wounded me more than I wanted to admit, mainly because of my pride and not wanting to acknowledge that a man I respected so little could wound me."

In the midst of his trauma, Winn turned to the Scriptures and found hope from the psalmists. He says they taught him that the spiritual life is one of anguish as well as hope. Though tempted to become cynical about his faith, Winn says he realized that cynicism just provides shortsighted relief. "Freedom is never found there," he says. "But only in wrestling and exploring and digging up all that has been covered by pain can true freedom be found."

Whether it is on the job or at home, hard times can and will hit you where it hurts the most. My friend Wendy had her life yanked out from under her shortly after the birth of her first child. Wendy's husband woke up one day, looked at her and their three-week-old son, and said, "This isn't the life I signed up for." He moved out, refused counseling, and filed for divorce. After five years of marriage, Wendy was a single mother.

"I'm only 27 years old," Wendy says. "I never, *ever* expected this to happen to me. My husband had always said to me that divorce was not an option, so his actions caught me completely off guard. There were days when I didn't think I could get out of bed to even nurse my son, but somehow, someway, God sustained me through it. I have learned what it means to rest in the shadow of His wings. I held on to Joseph's story and all that he went through and that he always said, 'God will use it for good.' I have clung to that and it has been helping me get through this." While the hurt, pain, and loss Wendy has to deal with are still very real, she is able to put her trust in the One who promises never to leave or forsake her (Hebrews 13:5).

No Longer Invincible

During my teens, I felt invincible—like I could do anything. Now that I am in my twenties, though, I am a little more realistic. I've been extremely blessed in my life, but my journey hasn't been without its share of hard times and hard landings. I've applied for a long list of colleges, universities, jobs, and publishing opportunities and received only stacks of rejection letters in reply. The mysterious death of a college friend in India and the death of a family member in a scuba-diving accident have shaken me to the very core of my being.

Last spring, I was so stressed out by my work and financial situation, I got sick every month for eight months in a row with whatever type of cold or flu was passing through town. On top of feeling terrible, the stress from juggling several jobs took such a toll on my body that I actually popped three ribs out of my spinal column, had a mysterious upper-abdomen pain that doctors couldn't identify, and had to be put on antidepressants for three months. I received a stern warning from my doctor that my body was trying to tell me something, and if I didn't listen and learn to slow down, something worse was going to happen. Talk about a wake-up call! I am gradually figuring out how to make healthy choices that allow me to live life with a little less stress and a lot bigger smile.

Sometimes hard times just happen—and it stinks. However, sometimes we bring them upon ourselves. Either way, it's not much fun. There are weeks and even months when I feel as if I'm a regular on *The Hard Times* delivery route. Fumbled relationships. Sickness. Loss. Broken promises. I've been rocked by hard times enough that the illusion of being invincible has worn off. Yet if I take a moment and compare my life to so many others', my hard times don't stack up too high. When I reflect on kids growing up without food or the grief of losing a loved one to a violent death, my hardship is transformed from white-capped waves to ripples.

But it's hard to have that kind of perspective when hard times are happening to you. When you're the one feeling the wave break over you—no matter what its height—it still tosses you around and causes pain. Hardship has also reminded me of the fragility of my being—physically, emotionally, and spiritually. Despite any pretenses that I am strong and have it all together, difficulty reminds me of my weaknesses and that I am desperately dependent on God.

I have read of many Christians who have faced hardship and then passionately shared their stories of triumph and grace in the midst of difficulty. But the stories that capture my heart are often those people who are living without Christ, but still testify to the results of hard times in their lives. Lance Armstrong, a multiple winner of the Tour-de-France, has made the profound statement that if he had to choose between winning the Tour-de-France and battling cancer, he'd choose the cancer every time. In his book, *It's Not about the Bike,* Armstrong attributes his race-winning strength to his battle with cancer and describes the deadly disease as "the best thing that ever happened to me."[1] In his autobiography, Michael J. Fox said he is "grateful" for having Parkinson's disease. Though he describes it as "the gift that keeps on taking," he says he has learned volumes about himself, his family, and life through the disease.[2]

Even without a professed Christian faith, these men have found hope in the midst of their heartache. Their stories remind me that it doesn't matter whether you're rich or poor or famous or unknown—everyone encounters hard times, including twentysomethings. As a believer, I should be at the front of the line, ahead of Lance Armstrong, Michael J. Fox, and others, embracing hope and love even in the midst of trials. But more often than not, I end up throwing a pity party for myself. I want to run, hide, duck, and do anything and everything to avoid those trials. It is a humbling and challenging idea that men who aren't able to share my eternal hope in Christ are able to take all the lemons the sinful world throws at them and still make lemonade.

Fingerprints of God

In the midst of hard times, I often have found the fingerprints of God's involvement—His mercy in a moment of tragedy. Last summer, my mom and I were attending my cousin's wedding celebration on one of the San Juan Islands off the coast of Washington. After participating in the joyous occasion, we parked our car in the holding area to catch the next ferry. We realized we had an extra five or ten minutes to spare and decided to head down to the nearby cabins for one final farewell to our family members. After all, it was the first time in more than thirty-five years that my mom and her two sisters had been together. It just made sense to capture every last moment.

As I sat chatting on the dock with my mother, my aunt Susan, my aunt Ruthie and her husband, Charles, and my cousins, the early morning breeze was cool, but the sun somehow kept us comfortable. The conversation was seasoned with laughter and warm memories. The five minutes grew into fifteen, which eventually grew into nearly an hour. The ferry was desperately late, but it seemed of little concern. Every so often, I looked at my watch and strained my neck to peek around the corner of the bay to see if the boat was on its way. There was no sign of it, and secretly I was grateful. It was one of those little precious moments in time.

Three days later I received a telephone call: Charles had been killed in a car accident leaving the parking lot of Wal-Mart. What followed was heartache beyond words, grief beyond expression, and pain that cut to the core of all our beings. There were many tears and much mourning. But even in the midst of the pain, I couldn't help but be grateful to God for those precious moments we were granted together before Charles was taken away.

I believe God tucks His strands of mercy and hope into every tragedy and heartache. Somehow, somewhere, He is still good to us. Often I don't see them until I'm past it, but then I realize they were there all along. The One who promises to work all things for good (Romans 8:28) is faithful. The "good" He is working may not be something I desire or recognize during this lifetime, but I believe God is true and that somewhere, maybe in eternity if not on earth, I will be able to fully recognize the good He has done in my life.

My friend Mike, a 29-year-old who received his master's from Azusa Pacific University, says he has come to terms with the fact that hard times are a normal part of life. "Of course they stink," he says. "But for the most part I think they should be embraced because it's the very thing God uses to make us stronger or weaker—whatever is necessary—to be the person we were meant to be."

Mike says he's gained many things through hard times, including humility, a sense of his depravity and insecurity, more about the faithfulness of God, a better understanding of grace, and a more thorough understanding of the validity, power, and relevance of the gospel. In addition, hard times have driven him to prayer and study. "My own spiritual discipline is usually lacking, but a fair amount of adversity keeps me plugged into Christ and continually seeking His will—as a survival instinct," he says. "I'm kind of afraid to say it, but perhaps adversity has been a good accountability partner."

Christine, a 30-year-old who works with the young adult ministry at Santa Cruz Bible Church, agrees and says young people are anything but immune to hardship. She would know. At 27 years old, Christine began dating one of the worship leaders at her church. The young man battled cancer for some time, but as their relationship grew, there were signs of remission. Soon after becoming engaged, the doctors discovered the cancer was growing through out his body and prescribed intense chemotherapy. Christine's fiancé reacted adversely to the treatment, and Christine spent the next few months caring for him when she wasn't working full-time at the church. I'd love to tell you that God healed this young man. But that didn't happen. And Christine held her fiancé in her arms as he died.

Christine says she has learned a lot from the pain she's gone through, though she's still processing much of it. She eventually took a five-month sabbatical from work and says she allowed herself to ask God the tough questions that plagued her. *Is God really a good God?* She struggled with core issues like why there are pain and suffering on earth and why she was permitted to go through this heartbreaking relationship when God already knew her fiancé was going to die. "During my time away, I was able to determine what was true," she says. "It became a deepening time for me and my relationship with God. It's so easy to go into denial and pretend this never happened. But deep down, the backdrop to my life was the ache of *Why, God?* But when it was just me and God alone, I was able to take time and deal with these issues head-on."

Though she recently returned from her sabbatical with a better grasp on some things, Christine says she is still wrestling with many issues and is slowly progressing in the healing process. Yet even in the midst of the pain, she is able to reach out and minister to others—those who have lost loved ones and experienced heartache. She says one of the main things she stresses to people who have experienced a tragedy or hardship is to give yourself permission to experience the loss in its entirety. "So many people feel that to be a Christian means you can't show signs of weakness or grief. You have to put on this zip-up suit, smiley face, and make sure you are joyful all the time. After my fiancé died, I felt that if I were to show people I was dying inside because of my loss, I was letting people down. I didn't want people to turn from God. If I could go back, I would cry when I needed to cry in front of people, get angry when I felt mad, question when I doubted, and ask for help when I really needed it. I would have given myself permission to be loved by the church. Strength doesn't come when we appear to have it all together. It comes when we are in desperate need and God uses His church to work things for the good."

Christine says there isn't a formula for dealing with hard times.

Those who are going through a difficult time need to try to knock down the conditioned walls of what they should or should not do, and who they need to be and when. "You may try to tell yourself that you should be over this in six months, but it may take you a year," she says. "Your process of healing isn't going to look like someone else's. Grief is messy. What satisfies my soul in these unknown facets of life is that although grief is messy, God preferred to use my life to tell about Jesus. My story is like no other. This gives me purpose."

◎   ◎   ◎

As you can probably tell, there are enough different kinds of hard times that everyone gets whacked with one at one time or another. Whether the biggest struggles you've faced are as minor as rejection or as major as death, I can confidently tell you that through it all, God is with you. He was with me when I decided to take all the responsibility of a low-paying, high-stress job on my shoulders instead of giving it to Him. My checkbook might still have had a balance in the red, but I know He was just waiting for me to come to Him for peace. I can tell you that my ribs are going to stay attached from now on—and the reason is simple: When I recognize that hard times are coming after me, I start praying and sharing my concerns and problems with Jesus. That doesn't make the problems go away, especially when they are a consequence of my own choices, but I find great comfort in knowing He is watching over me and helping me through them.

TWELVE SURVIVAL TIPS FOR HARD TIMES

1. *Remember, you are not alone in what you're experiencing.* Though the circumstances may differ, you're not the only one who has gone through this type of situation. Others have not only experienced it, they've survived it. And so will you.

2. *Find a Scripture promise.* Skip through the pages of the Bible and you'll find countless promises from God. There's even one for you. Maybe it's a verse you already know or one you've recently read. Write it down. Commit it to memory. And hold on to God's promises.

3. *Find a song or an album that encourages you.* Somewhere on the radio or in your CD library, there are lyrics that speak right to your situation. When you find them, hit "repeat" on your player.

4. *Talk to someone you can trust.* Hurting alone is dangerous business. Find someone who can compassionately relate and respond to what you're going through. Ask them to pray for you. You don't have to tell them every detail, but let them know, "I could really use your prayers."

5. *Consider spending time with a Christian counselor.* If your gray day doesn't seem to have an end but carries on for weeks or even months at a time, it's probably a good idea to seek professional help. Antidepressants can help lift the fog so you can reconnect with God and those around you.

6. *Get right with God.* Are there any areas of compromise in your life? Is there anything you feel God has asked you to do that you've left undone? Ask Him to reveal His purpose for this time in your life.

7. *Remember that this, too, will pass.* What you're going through or feeling isn't forever. Life is a series of seasons, and this one has a sunrise, even if you can't see it.

8. *Know your limits.* Events will naturally arise that will tempt you to fill your schedule and spread yourself too thin. Learn to say no.

9. *Go on a road trip.* It's time to visit a friend in a nearby city, buy a plane ticket, or take a vacation. Getting out of the situation you're in will allow you to acquire a fresh perspective.

10. *Sleep.* Going through tough times is emotionally taxing. It takes a toll on your body. You probably need more sleep than usual. Find ways to get it. Skip unnecessary meetings or gatherings.

11. *Once you're rested, get out of the house.* Go to the movies, grab dinner with a friend, or attend a sporting event. Being around others will lift your spirit.

12. *Give yourself a treat.* When you're feeling down, it's easy to forget to take care of yourself and your needs. Splurge on a fancy lunch out with a close friend. Sign up for a thirty-minute back massage. Take a day off and spend it reading in the park. Remember to celebrate life.

FAST FACTS

→ Moving In: According to the National Association of Realtors, the median age of the first-time homebuyer has been dropping, from age 32 in 1999 to age 31 in 2001. The number of sales from those under 25 rose from 305,192 in 1999 to 321,136 in 2001. ("More 30-Year Mortgages for Twenty-somethings," *St. Petersburg Times,* February 2, 2003.)

→ Big Savers: Twentysomethings are far more intent on saving for retirement than their parents were. Among 18- to 34-year-olds, 24 percent started saving for retirement before they turned 20, whereas only 4 percent of people 50 and older started saving that young. (Jeff Brown, "Twentysomethings Don't Need to Save at Expense of Fun," Knight Ridder/ Tribune News Service, February 22, 1999.)

from surviving to thriving

A lot has changed since I made the initial break from my teens to the twenties. I think I've fallen into a nice rhythm in life, though. I work, sleep, eat, hang out with cool people, spend time with God, and even pay my bills on time. Life is pretty good. I no longer wonder where to take my car when it breaks down or where the money is coming from for next month's rent. I feel blessed and grateful.

Several years ago, I ran the Elerby Springs Marathon in the foothills of North Carolina. (If you've never heard of it, don't worry, neither had I.) As far as I can remember, there were only eighty-seven contestants, so you can wipe any pictures of the glorious moments you've seen on television of the Ironman Triathlon or the Boston Marathon from your mind. In this small race, water stations were few and far between, and the whispers of wind and tall waving grass replaced cheering crowds alongside the road.

I had two specific goals for my first marathon: I didn't want to come in last, and I wanted to run the entire way. Around mile twelve, a fellow racer twisted her ankle, and I knew I was going to accomplish at least one of my goals. As far as the other goal was concerned, I knew there were some people who would probably testify that running and waddling are not the same thing, but I counted anything with even a hint of a bounce as part of a jog, which is in the same category as a run.

Marathon runners all talk about *hitting the wall*—that point in the race when you think you can't go any farther. Most people hit the wall around mile twenty. I hit the wall around mile thirteen. It was hot, I was tired, and I didn't know if I was going to make it to the finish line. So I joggled (a fine blend of walking, waddling, and jogging all at the same time) my way through the next few miles, trying to think about anything other than the aches and blisters. Around mile nineteen, I saw another competitor in the distance. Only he wasn't running or even waddling, he was walking. I reminded myself, *I won't come in next to last if I can keep going!* I felt exhilarated as I passed the exhausted competitor, so I set my eyes on the next runner, and then the one after that. My joggle became a legitimate jog and eventually qualified as a running pace. My legs felt as if they were on autopilot, beating out a steady pace on the hot, black pavement. During the last six miles of the race, I passed dozens of competitors and even beat one additional racer in a sprint to the finish line. I received a third-place award for women in my age category. Granted, there were only a total of four women in my age bracket, but I accepted the engraved prize with satisfaction anyway.

Running a marathon was near the top of my lifelong to-do list, and completing that 26.2-mile race carried an incredible sense of accomplishment. Now if you had asked me how I felt between miles thirteen and sixteen, I wouldn't have given the same report. That's because sometimes it's hard to appreciate something when you're still in the middle of it. Like the miles of a marathon, some of the twentysomething years are better than others. That first year out of school can be pretty bumpy, and any time in life that involves a crisis can be difficult, too. Yet when you stand back and look at these twentysomething years, there's little doubt that they are designed to be some of the best of your life.

THE SEVEN WONDERS OF THE TWENTYSOMETHING WORLD

Interested? You're probably expecting a clever use of metaphors that relates life in your twenties to the Seven Wonders of the Ancient World. Well, that isn't going to happen. Those wonders are mostly gone—destroyed by time and man—and if I were writing this book in my thirties, I could probably pull it off because I'd be looking back into the past. Instead, I'm writing in the midst of some of the most enjoyable and challenging experiences I've faced in all my years. I don't know if you have experienced these yet, but when you start evaluating your life—where it's been, compared to where it's going—some thoughts and concepts really stick out. So, without further ado (drumroll, please), here is a list of the Seven Wonders of the Twentysomething World:

1. Options, Freedom, and Flexibility

During your twenties, you have unlimited opportunities. Many choices are available. You can choose where you want to live, what you want to do, and in whom you want to invest time. You can experiment. I mean, come on—it just makes sense to try new things. If you don't do it now, when will you?

"The absolute best part of being 24 and single is that my life is an open book! I can go and do whatever I choose; the paths and roads are endless," says Kelly, one passionate twentysomething. "I am free to go and do whatever I want right now and explore any career path I want. It's such a great feeling to know that I can live out all my dreams right now without anyone or anything holding me back!"

Jill, a 27-year-old small-animal veterinarian in Connecticut, says she feels that she still has time to switch careers if her current one doesn't work out. "I feel as though I still have a lot of living, learning, and growing to do . . . and still have plenty of pre-children time in my marriage," she says.

No matter what career path you might take, you still have the option of changing. You can be an administrative assistant one day and work with disabled children the next. Where the next mortgage payment is coming from doesn't really matter because you are sharing a one-bedroom apartment with three other people. Just like job opportunities, roommates and housing change a lot in your twenties. From living in a studio to sharing a five-bedroom house with a pool, no matter where you are sleeping, chances are it will change during the next year. That's what being in your twenties is all about—exploring the options and finding out what is really important to you.

2. A Great Time for Travel and Exploration!

Living in Alaska, I see a lot of people with canes and wheelchairs pulling their oxygen supply tank along to enjoy the last frontier. How much better would their memories be if they were able to say that they had hiked a glacier or kayaked with whales? Instead, their memories consist of sitting on a bus and hearing about what other people have done in Alaska. In your twenties, you can go backpacking in Europe for months on end. Hopefully, you'll still be able to do that when you're fifty, but for right now you've got a lot less holding you down, and your knees will still hold up to a hike.

You also have the energy, strength, and wherewithal to travel on a shoestring budget. You can explore new areas of the country and the world. You can still crash on people's floors and couches and get by on salami and crackers if you want. You can fly to Boston to see friends or spend the weekend at someone's lake house on a moment's notice. You may like the idea of a four-star resort, but you're still willing to stay in a one- or two-star hotel if it means getting to see new sights or visit a new city. You can take advantage of travel opportunities through work or a fellowship opportunity to study or work abroad.

Ellen, a 29-year-old graduate of the University of North Carolina, has traveled to Spain, Germany, and Switzerland and backpacked at Glacier National Park. She has tried paragliding, metalwork, snowboarding, road biking, and rock climbing. Reflecting, Ellen says, "I think one of the most important things to me in my twenties has been experimentation with life. I have moved several times, traveled, loved and lost, read incredible life-shaping literature, tried new sports and arts, and, most important, made wonderful female friends. I would recommend the same to anyone else, especially to women in their twenties. Try it out. Figure out your strengths and weaknesses. Take time to determine what is the correct path for you instead of accepting the path that others lay out for you."

You can discover new cities, towns, people, and schools. You can refine your skills and giftings as you embrace life. You can also test new ideas. You can come to terms with what you believe to be true and take time to study and have ready answers to questions about what you believe. You've been raised with a certain set of values, and in your twenties, you can evaluate whether to make those beliefs your own or make adjustments. You can grow into your own skin with an understanding of your personal beliefs and faith.

3. Time to Learn

Contrary to what some commencement speakers might tell you, the learning process doesn't end with graduation. In fact, it's just getting started. Through all the trials and tribulations, successes and failures, you are learning something new every day. You are learning about yourself, the world around you, and how to thrive in it. Depending on the choices you make, you can either slowly ease your way into the mire of adult responsibility or throw caution to the wind and jump in with both feet.

Your twenties are a great time to try to put your ideals into practice. You can test them and find out which actually work and which really don't. You can make life choices and develop life patterns. You have more wisdom based on your experience than you did in school, but you haven't lost the desire to try new things for yourself. You can find your passions and find yourself as you discover new things.

One of the best things about being in your twenties is that pretty much anyone will help you. If you need a mentor, someone to encourage you or help you out, people are often more than willing to lend a listening ear, comforting shoulder, or helping hand. As one twentysomething pointed out, "Now's the time to ask, before you become the competition."

Oh, yeah, and you can still be silly. You can play paint ball or laser tag and build potato guns. Even if you don't have a kid, you can still act like one. Look for any opportunities to have some fun, learn something, and get out there and enjoy it.

4. Energy and Youth

The twentysomething years have a youthful vibrancy. There are an excitement and hope that permeate every fiber of our being. You can use that energy to accomplish personal goals, and if you can't change the world, at least you can change the world around you.

Shane, a 31-year-old living in Los Angeles, says that youth is to be treasured and enjoyed. "For some reason, good or bad, it's still okay to screw up," she says. "It's okay to try everything within God's eyes before you have to settle down or be responsible. Yes, you should learn to invest, register your car on time, have an occasional blood test, watch your sodium intake—but don't forgo the opportunity to hold on to your immature youth. Pull a fun prank on your friends, backpack Europe on $5 a day, meet everyone you can—just because."

Shane says one of the things she's most proud of is that she's never missed a trip or chance to travel or do something crazy. She keeps a set of envelopes in her dresser drawer labeled for all the different trips she's planned: one for summer graduate school in Vermont, another for the Nantucket Film Festival where she entered a screenplay, and another for a trip to Africa to document the AIDS crisis.

"If I didn't have enough money at any given point, no fret, I'd find an odd job and get it," she says. "Nothing stood in my way of going places and visiting all my friends every year. Granted, I never thought of saving for a condo or a 401(k) or getting a dental plan, but I sure never missed out on something cool."

5. New Relationships and Friendships

For some, those new relationships include marriage, while for others, they include developing strong friendships and a sense of community. During your twenties, you can form friendships that will last a lifetime.

After moving back to Colorado, I became established with a group of amazing friends. Not just any ordinary group of friends—we were The Tribe. From all over the United States, with diverse backgrounds and some pretty amazing experiences in our pasts, we were joined together by our love for Christ and a desire for deeper relationships. I started as an individual in a new city, and by the time I left, I was part of a group of brothers and sisters in Christ that goes beyond anything I ever would have imagined. I have moved around a bit since those days, but that group of friends continues to hold me accountable and share both my joys and my tears.

The twenties are an amazing time to reach out to others and serve them. Brian Habig, chaplain for Reformed University Fellowship at Vanderbilt University, notes that twentysomethings are afforded a tremendous amount of freedom by God. "Harness it for the good of another," he says. "If you don't know where to serve, just look at wherever God has placed you. Of all the places you could be, He put you there! Begin looking around, and if you want to serve, you won't have to look long."

6. The Start of Incredible Adventures

Life as an adult is just beginning, and you can do anything. The doors are wide open as far as choices and opportunities, and it feels adventurous. There is expectancy, a sense that just about anything might be around the next corner. You can wake up one day and do something entirely different with your life. You have tremendous potential. Your whole life is still ahead of you.

Shelley, a 23-year-old graduate of the University of Tennessee, says, "There is so much freedom. People are still moving and traveling. Most of my friends have not settled down yet. There is always this feeling of expectancy. Things could be entirely different next year. This time last year, I had no idea my life would look like this. It could be the same next year."

I know people who say high school was the best time in their lives. Whether they were the star of the football team or the prettiest girl in school, it really doesn't matter to them what they do after graduation because they think that the good years of their lives are behind them. I don't want to be so shortsighted. I want my twenties, thirties, forties, and on up, even until age 90-plus, to be wonderful. That means I have to make some good choices now. I figure if I take a few less mogul runs at the ski area now, I can go skiing with my grandkids later. My knees are good for only so many bumpy black diamond runs. Of course, since I won't be skydiving at 80, I'll probably need to start planning that adventure now.

7. A Wonderful Time to Grow in Your Relationship with God

This is one of the best parts of being in your twenties. For those who are single or don't have children yet, this is an incredible age to make time to spend with God. It's also a time to grow in your relationship with Him.

Katie, a 23-year-old graduate of Mississippi State University, says, "This time has helped shake up my selfishness and made me really think about what I want the life I have been given to look like. I know God is teaching me much and growing my relationship with Him through this."

Gillian, a 24-year-old living outside Decatur, Georgia, says she feels that God is showing her ways she can serve others that she hadn't thought of before. "We have great fellowship, and I love hanging out with kid-less couples whom I can be real and honest with—it is neat to share with other couples who are going through the same things," she says. "I feel God is showing me that my two main purposes in life are to love Him and love others. I had previously thought that spending time with others took away from my devotion to Christ, but I am beginning to realize that is His entire purpose for me—to love the body of Christ as He has loved me."

Gillian says she feels she can serve her friends through sharing feelings and being open and honest about struggles in marriage, work, and life. "I have received the gift of open and honest friends who make me feel normal about my life, so I feel I can serve others by stripping away superficiality and engaging in real fellowship by revealing my sinfulness and need for Christ," she says. "This is hard for me, but I know that by sharing burdens, the Christian life is so much more full and fellowship is just more real."

Like many twentysomethings, my own twenties have been and

still are full of adventure, trials, rewards, relationships, broken hearts, tears, laughter, pain, questions, bliss, and love. Though I make a lot of mistakes, I can look forward to seeing how God will carry me through. His grace is so intriguing. It's all the hardships, mistakes, wonders, and joys that have contributed to who I am today.

As one twentysomething observed, "Being in your twenties is suspenseful—like watching a fireworks show on the Fourth of July. The possibilities are endless."

A FINAL WORD ABOUT THE TWENTYSOMETHING YEARS

You never know what's going to happen during your twenties. I think back about the motley crew that Jesus called to be His disciples. Bible scholars estimate that many of them were in their teens and twenties when they were invited to follow Jesus. Did those fishermen and young professionals ever expect such an opportunity? No way. But God had some great things in store for them. Just as He has great things in store for you and me.

A few years ago my uncle died, and my aunt needed an extra hand running their bed-and-breakfast for a few weeks during the summer. So I flew to Sitka, Alaska, and spent several weeks serving her guests fresh scones and sharing information about a little town I barely knew myself. I had an incredible time, and when my aunt invited me to return a second summer, I booked my plane ticket six months in advance. While in Sitka, I was invited to sign books at a local church. An extremely tall Norwegian man came by the signing table and purchased two copies. Later, he invited me to spend time with his group of friends. I accepted, and a friendship was born that grew into a long-lasting relationship.

Months later, we went for a hike. We had walked a short way on the trail when I noticed a long-stemmed red rose along the path with a homemade card in a hand-stamped envelope. I opened it and read the kind words of affirmation and love that were written inside. We continued along the trail, and there was another long-stemmed red rose and handmade card. The roses and cards continued for the entire two-mile hike until I had collected an enormous bouquet. Then, we came to a park bench overlooking the water. The bench held another dozen roses and a wooden bowl, which held a diamond ring. Alongside the bowl was a bath towel and some fragrant oil. Leif got down on one knee and proposed, and I said, "Yes." He proceeded to wash my feet and express his desire to love, serve, and affirm me for the rest of my life. After praying together, he took me out to an incredible five-star dinner at my favorite restaurant. I used to think that God gave good things to those who waited, but now I know that He doesn't just give us good things—He gives the very best. And I am more excited and joyful than words can express.

It's impossible to know the mind or heart of God and all the good things He has stored up for us. Sometimes they include friendships. Sometimes they include accountability. Sometimes they include newfound love. And sometimes they include wonderful surprises.

If you can't tell by now, there's a lot to look forward to and enjoy in the twentysomething years. Sure, there may be a few issues with creditors and roommates that might try to get in the way and drag you down, but they really are small in the big scheme of things. The problems will be only as big as you allow them to become, and the joys will be only as obvious as you choose to be aware of them. The twentysomething years are about figuring out who you are and really defining your identity, purpose, gifts, and callings, and those aren't the kind of issues you can figure out on a weekend retreat or in a few months of living on a shoestring budget in Europe. No, those kinds of questions take a lot longer, sometimes a decade or more to figure out. And just for the record, the conclusions you draw now will probably change. Buckle up and get ready for the ride of your life. God is going to use everything that happens for His glory and so you can learn to rely on Him. God loves you, so get out and enjoy your twentysomething years!

PSALM 31:14–15

But I trust in you, O LORD; I say, "You are my God." My times are in your hands.

thirtysomething

For a number of years, I couldn't even say the word *thirty*. And anyone who was truly my friend knew well enough not to mention the word around me, at least when it was in reference to me. Sure, they could talk about themselves turning 30 or someone they knew already being 30. But for the most part, that word was off-limits whenever I was around. I secretly thought if I avoided acknowledging the word, I could avoid the experience all together. I was wrong.

As much as I fought it, my birthday came around each year, and there was nothing I could do to stop it. So when I turned 29, I knew that in a short twelve months I finally would have to come to grips with growing older. I'd like to tell you that I didn't freak out or I took it calmly or it was a walk in the park. But it wasn't.

Rather than freak out about turning thirty, I went ahead and freaked out at the big 2-9. I spent an entire month freaking out. I had my hair done, purchased new outfits, went on a rapid-weight-loss plan, and shed a quick eight pounds. In the end, I felt great. The best part about freaking out early is that when it's your thirtieth birthday, you can actually enjoy it!

So what happens when the big 3-0 hits? Many thirtysomethings say they begin to find their groove. They find a rhythm in life that is apparent as they handle work, relationships, and faith with a finesse and familiarity they didn't have during their twenties. Shane, who recently celebrated her thirty-first birthday, says she's ignoring the fact that she's no longer a twentysomething and still pretending she's 26. "People respect my opinion now, even though they're not quite sure how old I am," she says. "But one thing is for sure—I'm more confident and happy with me, my clothes, the world."

She says that in the course of living, however, she's lost the care-freeness she had a few short years ago. "I feel the pressure to buy, not rent," she says. "I wonder about my future retirement plan once in a while. I get more afraid of people I love dying. I'm more aware of my gums, my hair color, oil changes, good credit, skin cancer, little kids running out into the street, looking professional at a meeting, the phone bill, and long-lost childhood friends. In some ways I wish I were 24—now, that was a great year."

Jared Mackey, a 29-year-old pastor at the Next Level Church in Denver, Colorado, says those who often want to conquer the world in their youth will find their goals changing as they progress through their twenties. "It's hard to determine whether we are set-tling for less or if we're coming to a healthy understanding of our place," he says. "It's not that we don't still have the desire, but maybe the world we have desired to conquer has changed or grown smaller. Priorities have shifted. As a messiah-complex young adult who grew up in a church, I wanted to be a director of Promise Keepers for younger guys and see stadiums full of people because that's what I believe is important. But the fact that I have ten to twenty people in my home every Sunday is just as important as or more important than filling a stadium. The things I once found more important have shifted."

So don't be afraid of the big, bad 3-0. During your thirties, you can expect to continue growing, changing, and falling into a healthy rhythm of life.

FREEBIES

SURIVIVING YOUR FIRST CHRISTMAS (OR ANY MAJOR HOLIDAY) AWAY FROM HOME

I knew for months that I wasn't going to spend Christmas with my family, but it didn't become reality until I attended a Sunday morning church service in late December. Interspersed between worship songs were familiar holiday choruses. Christmas trees decorated with ornaments and lights stood brightly at the front of the church. Staring into the lights and limbs of a decorated tree, I realized that Christmas—the holiday I had shared with my family for twenty-some years—was only two days away, and my family was on the other side of the country. Hidden emotions tucked deep inside my soul began to stir as my eyes moistened. I tried to hold back the tears by widening my eyes and creating a greater surface tension so they couldn't fall, but it was no use. They fell anyway.

A young girl was hanging in her father's arms in the row in front of me. Her penetrating big brown eyes wouldn't veer. She watched every tear fall. After a few more songs, the children were finally dismissed from the service. I slipped out of the church during the transition and headed for my car. I had to go somewhere, anywhere. I drove a few miles before realizing there was nowhere to go and pulled off into the McDonald's parking lot and cried and prayed and prayed and cried. My soul eventually settled down, and I drove home feeling slightly relieved but sad.

Christmas away from home is never easy, but your first Christmas away from family is by far the hardest. Later in the day, I called one of my best friends from college. It had been a hard year for her. Her husband had an affair and left her with their six-week-old baby to raise on her own. The tough days and long nights as a single mom were exhausting, and now as the holidays approached, she was confronted with her singleness and potentially engulfing sense of loneliness.

Despite the struggles and obstacles she faced, there was hope in her voice. "You know, I have every reason to be down this holiday season," she confessed. "But I'm not. I realize that Christmas isn't about me. It's not about what I want or my little traditions or any of this man-made stuff. Christmas is about the birth of Jesus. Period. Nothing more. And as long as I keep my eyes on that truth—that it's all about Him—this is much easier to get through."

She was living an eternal truth: When we place our eyes on Christ instead of on ourselves, our perception changes. I realized that my sadness was a result of focusing on one person—me. Christmas isn't my birthday; it's Christ's birthday, and He's the One I need to focus on. He is a reason to celebrate. Even when it's with strangers. Even when I'm a few thousand miles from home. Even when I can't partake in all the family traditions.

So if you find yourself away from home for the first time, surround yourself with people who love and appreciate you. Try to introduce one or two of your own traditions to your new friends—even if it's as simple as telling a story or baking a particular type of pie. And make sure to carve out time to call your loved ones. They miss you just as much, if not more, than you miss them!

MAINTAINING FRIENDSHIPS FROM MILES AWAY

I've moved eight times in the last seven years. I've lived in North Carolina, Florida, Colorado, and Alaska, and along the way I've made some pretty incredible friends. I can't keep track of them all, but many of them are just too good to let go. You probably have some of them, too. So here are a few tips on how to maintain friendships, even when the miles try to keep you away.

1. Pick Up the Phone and Call

Long distance used to be expensive. Not anymore. Calling cards from mass wholesalers like Costco and Sam's Club have brought long-distance calls down to under four cents a minute. That means a twenty-minute catch-up call costs less than a buck. So if you want to spend an hour on the phone getting all the details, you're still way under the cost of an iced mocha at Starbucks. A lot of cell phone carriers provide unlimited night and weekend minutes, so you can catch up with old college friends for free. On weekends, I usually take a walk with my cell phone and call my friends. That way I get exercise and maintain friendships at the same time.

2. Stock Up on Cards

Every few months, I buy a stack of note cards and jot messages to friends while watching some reruns on television. The notes aren't excessively long, and they don't take a lot of time, but they help people know I still care.

3. Don't Underestimate the Value of a Postcard

Postcards provide a short, quick way to let someone know you're thinking of them. So the next time you're on a trip, buy a stack and send them to loved ones.

4. E-Mail and Instant Messages

The Internet is a great way to keep in touch with people. It's instant and it's easy.

5. The Friendship Ball

A few years ago, I received a little friendship ball. It's a silver ball that's meant to be exchanged between two people with a gift and a note. I gave it to my neighbor Sheila with a chocolate bar and a pasta strainer she desperately needed at the time. It came back with some fun fluffy slippers and a card. Since 1999, the ball has made dozens of trips back and forth between us, reminding each of us of our friendship.

6. Last-Minute Trips

The next time airline prices take a dip, consider hopping on a plane to go visit old friends. Or if a flight isn't available, consider going on an extended road trip. Stay with people you know along the way. It's amazing how a visit—even if it's only for a day—can strengthen a friendship.

MOVING BACK IN WITH THE FAM

It takes time for parents to get used to having an empty nest, a home without children. But just about the time they're getting settled into their quiet homestead, we're back! Most of the time, it's finances that drive us back to Mom and Dad. We need to save up enough for the first and last months' rent, a set of four wheels, and a little padding, just in case something goes wrong. Oh, and we also need to figure out what we're going to do with our lives. Fortunately, most parents are happy to oblige.

But moving back in with the "'rents" isn't always easy. Here's a few things to make the transition go a lot smoother:

→ As soon as you move in (and preferably before), have a talk with your parents about each of your expectations. What are your responsibilities (financial contributions, cooking, cleaning, chores, etc.)? And what are their responsibilities?

→ Talk about the house rules. Which guidelines from your youth do your parents still expect you to obey? Do they expect you to be home by a certain time? Do they expect you to tell them where you're going? Find out which, if any, rules your parents still want to keep and determine whether you can live with them.

→ Always define the length of time you want to stay. Even if you don't know an absolute date, set a time frame, whether it's three or six months or longer, to avoid any miscommunication.

→ Develop a system for working through issues that naturally arise when people live together. Open communication is key to a smooth living arrangement. Consider picking a night of the week or a note board on which to address issues of frustration, anxiety, or stress.

ENCOURAGING SCRIPTURE

Now to him who is able to do immeasurably more than all we ask or imagine, according to his power that is at work within us, to him be glory in the church and in Christ Jesus throughout all generations, for ever and ever! Amen. (Ephesians 3:20–21)

Being confident of this, that he who began a good work in you will carry it on to completion until the day of Christ Jesus. (Philippians 1:6)

You hear, O LORD, the desire of the afflicted; you encourage them, and you listen to their cry. (Psalm 10:17)

For we do not have a high priest who is unable to sympathize with our weaknesses, but we have one who has been tempted in every way, just as we are—yet was without sin. Let us then approach the throne of grace with confidence, so that we may receive mercy and find grace to help us in our time of need. (Hebrews 4:15–16)

Surely I am with you always, to the very end of the age. (Matthew 28:20)

So then, just as you received Christ Jesus as Lord, continue to live in him, rooted and built up in him, strengthened in the faith as you were taught, and overflowing with thankfulness. (Colossians 2:6–7)

But now, this is what the LORD says—he who created you, O Jacob, he who formed you, O Israel: "Fear not, for I have redeemed you; I have summoned you by name; you are mine. When you pass through the waters, I will be with you; and when you pass through the rivers, they will not sweep over you. When you walk through the fire, you will not be burned; the flames will not set you ablaze. For I am the LORD, your God, the Holy One of Israel, your Savior." (Isaiah 43:1–3)

Do not let your heart envy sinners, but always be zealous for the fear of the LORD. There is surely a future hope for you, and your hope will not be cut off. (Proverbs 23:17–18)

But blessed is the man who trusts in the LORD, whose confidence is in him. He will be like a tree planted by the water that sends out its roots by the stream. It does not fear when heat comes; its leaves are always green. It has no worries in a year of drought and never fails to bear fruit. (Jeremiah 17:7–8)

LOW-FAT SNACK OPTIONS (TO AVOID THE AFOREMENTIONED "SECRETARY SPREAD")

→ Munch on a handful of pretzels.

→ Slice up your favorite fruits and try freezing them. Bananas, peaches, grapes, and other fresh fruits are delicious and refreshing when frozen.

→ Spread some reduced-calorie peanut butter on a rice cake.

→ Buy a low-calorie protein bar. Steer clear of the hefty, 250-plus-calorie ones.

→ Gum. Okay, this isn't a snack, but sometimes it works!

→ Make yourself a salad.

→ Eat a few hard-boiled eggs.

→ Have a can of tuna (the dolphin-friendly kind, of course).

→ Enjoy an afternoon bowl of cereal with skim milk.

→ Pop some light microwave popcorn.

→ Cut up some carrots, celery, and other munchable veggies. Skip the ranch dressing.

→ Grab a handful of baked potato chips.

→ Have a bowl of sugar-free Jell-O or pudding.

→ Grab a cup of coffee or tea and biscotti.

NINE TOUGH JOB INTERVIEW QUESTIONS AND HOW TO ANSWER THEM

Don't want to flub on your next job interview? Me neither. Here are nine commonly asked questions that can throw you for a loop.

1. Tell Us about Yourself

Many people have difficulty with this question because it seems too broad and too difficult to get one's hands on the meat of the question. Do you talk about your personality, work skills, hobbies, family goals, or outside activities? Where do you start?

It is important to keep in mind that you are in the interview to discuss business—and only business—unless otherwise directed. All answers should be given in a businesslike manner. Therefore, the summary of experience from your résumé is the perfect response for this answer, which should be between fifteen and twenty seconds in length.

2. What Are Your Short-Range Objectives?

Before attempting to answer, you would be extremely prudent to have a definition of the vocabulary. They seem so obvious, but what would be your response if you thought short-range

objectives were only one or two years, and the manager or inter-
viewer was looking for a response of three to five years? Ask for a
definition of "short" so the answer can reflect the proper time
frame.

3. What Can You Do for Us That Someone Else Cannot Do?

This question asks you to compare yourself with an unknown,
and since you cannot address the unknown, you will need to
remove the unknown from the answer. You should reconsider the
secret recipe question, "What is the company looking for in the successful candidate?" Find out what the company is looking for and
then resell yourself to its specific need.

4. How Good Is Your Health?

Your health is excellent. A human resource hiring official or
hiring manager is not a doctor, and it is not his or her role to inter-
pret the status of your physical condition. If, in the interview
process, the health question is probed further, and you have had a
health problem, offer to take a company physical and let a doctor
evaluate your health. Do not offer information about your health
that could possibly be damaging to your career.

5. What Kind of Salary Are You Worth?

In all salary questions, your first basic response should be that
you are open. You want to avoid a number. The minute you start to
discuss salary in terms of numbers, you start to close the sale.
Preclosure of a sale can destroy the sale. Remember, with the reply
"Open," you are saying that you are open to listen to a competitive
offer.

6. What Is Your Biggest Strength? Weakness?

When stating your biggest strengths, you should again refer to your résumé or reiterate one or more of your most current significant accomplishments. Discussing areas of weakness can lead an applicant to talk too much, pontificate, and give information that could be devastating to his or her campaign. In the area of weakness, state that sometimes you are "too hardworking," pay "too much attention to detail," and are "too critical" of your work. Who would not want to hire someone who is hardworking, pays attention to detail, or is critical of his or her work?

7. How Long Would You Stay with Us?

A simple response could be, "I would stay with the organization as long as I can continue to grow in my career."

8. What Position Do You Expect to Have in Five Years?

Be careful. It is suggested that you do not use a specific title. Instead, use an area; for example, you should not answer with "vice president" or "manager" of a certain area, because that position may not exist. A better way to handle this would be to say, "After I am in my position, I hope that my accomplishments will be recognized, and I will be promoted upward to either a supervisory or management position," if that is your career goal or objective.

9. How Would You Describe Your Personality?

Since most of us are not psychologists, this could be a very difficult question. Many individuals basically destroy themselves when asked this question. A suggested answer is, "My personality is very complex." When you are in the role of a person directly managed by a supervisor, you may want to say, "I try to be a very cooperative, flexible individual." If you are a manager, you may answer, "I try to be a very thorough individual, supportive of those who work for me."

Adapted from Lawrence A. Stuenkel, *From Here to There: A Self-Paced Program for Transition in Employment,* 5th ed. (Tempe, AZ: Facts on Demand Press, 2002), 283–305. Used with permission of author.

Introduction

1. Denis Howe, ed., *The Free On-Line Dictionary of Computing,* www.foldoc.org. If you would like to read the best of the best urban legends, About.com hosts its own list of the top twenty-five urban legends. It's worth a little Web surfing for a laugh or two.

2. Janelle Erlichman, "Life after Graduation: It Goes On and It's Good," *Washington Post,* May 29, 2001.

Chapter One

1. Sandra Block, "Student Loan Interest Rates Headed below 4%," *USA Today,* May 7, 2003.

2. According to findings by the National Survey of Families and Households as well as the U.S. Census Bureau as quoted in Laurence Roy Stains, "Look Who's Back," *AARP,* March/April 2003, 27; and "Boomerang Kids: Strategies for the Not-So-Empty Nest" at www.healthyworkplaces.com/images/boomerangkids.pdf.

Chapter Two

1. Dr. Seuss, *Oh, the Places You'll Go! The Unique Challenges of Life in Your Twenties* (New York: Random House, 1990), 2, 11.

2. Alexandra Robbins and Abby Wilner, *Quarterlife Crisis* (Los Angeles: J. P. Tarcher, 2001), 3.

3. Stacy Humes-Schulz, "Suffering the Quarterlife Crisis," *Daily Pennsylvanian*, July 26, 2001.

4. Sarah Skidmore, "If You're This Age, You Know the Angst Associated with the Quarterlife Crisis," Jacksonville.com, June 24, 2001.

5. Chris Penitila, "Generational Gyrations," *Entrepreneur,* April 2001, 102.

6. Henry Cloud and John Townsend, *How People Grow: What the Bible Reveals about Personal Growth* (Grand Rapids: Zondervan, 2001), 32. The "Serenity Prayer" reads, "God, give us grace to accept with serenity the things that cannot be changed, courage to change the things which should be changed, and the wisdom to distinguish the one from the other" (Reinhold Niebuhr, 1943).

7. From www.canadian-health-network.ca (accessed March 13, 2003).

8. Norman Wright, interview, Spring 2003.

Chapter Three

1. Revelation 3:12 tells us, "I will write on him the name of my God and the name of the city of my God, the new Jerusalem, which is coming down out of heaven from my God; and I will also write on him my new name."

2. Norman Wright, interview, Spring 2003.

3. Frederica Matthews-Greene, "A Clear and Present Identity," *Christianity Today,* September 4, 2000, 114. Used with permission of author.

4. Andy Crouch, interview, Spring 2003.

5. Kurt Warner, *Today's Christian Woman,* January/February 2003, 14, on-line version. Used with permission of publisher.

6. Matthew Woodley, "How I Came to Terms with My Role in the Church," *Leadership Journal,* summer 1999. Used with permission of author.

7. For more on your identity in Christ, I highly recommend on-line resources that offer lists of Bible verses describing our identity in Christ. For a game to help you memorize these Scriptures, visit www.camarillosda.org/games/inchrist/index.html.

8. The Myers-Briggs test can also help you determine a career path. Christian books including *Spirit-Controlled Temperament* by Tim LaHaye (Wheaton, IL: Tyndale House, 1993); and *Personality Plus: How to Understand Others by Understanding Yourself* by Florence Littauer (Grand Rapids: Revell Books, 1992) will prove extremely helpful.

9. Dan Kimball, interview, Spring 2003.

10. Craig Brian Larson, gen. ed., *More Perfect Illustrations for Every Topic and Occasion* (Wheaton, IL: Tyndale House), 301–2.

11. Ken Baugh and Rich Hurst, *The Quest for Christ: Discipling Today's Young Adults* (Loveland, CO: Group Publishing, 2002).

Chapter Four

1. Gloria May Stoddard, *Snowflake Bentley: Man of Science, Man of God* (Shelburne: New England Press), 33–34.

2. Ibid., 93.

3. Dois I. Rosser Jr. and Ellen Vaughn, *The God Who Hung on the Cross* (Grand Rapids: Zondervan, 2003), 140. Used with permission of publisher.

Chapter Five

1. Taken from Ravi Zacharias's address to the United Nations Prayer Breakfast on September 10, 2002. To read the entire speech, visit www.gospelcom.net/rzim/publications/essay_arttext.php?id=13.

2. Cloud and Townsend, *How People Grow*.

3. For more information, visit www.kairosonline.org.

4. "Boomerang Kids: Strategies for the Not-So-Empty Nest," at www.healthyworkplaces.com/images/boomerangkids.pdf.

5. Lori Smith, interview, 2003.

6. Cari Stone, "Forgoing Dink Status," posted November 8, 2002, at www.relevantmagazine.com. http://www.relevantmagazine.com/ modules.php?op=modload&name=News&file=article&sid=664. Used with permission of author.

7. John Towsend, interview.

8. Ajith Fernando, *Jesus Driven Ministry* (Wheaton, IL: Crossway Books, 2002), 48.

9. Taken from Ravi Zacharias's address to the United Nations Prayer Breakfast on September 10, 2002. To read the entire speech, visit www.gospelcom.net/rzim/publications/essay_arttext.php?id=13.

10. Andrew Murray, *An Exciting New Life* (New Kensington: Whitaker House, 1982).

11. John Ruhlman, interview, 2003.

Chapter Six

1. Lance Armstrong, *It's Not about the Bike: My Journey Back to Life* (New York: Berkley, 2001).

2. Michael J. Fox, *Lucky Man: A Memoir* (Winnipeg: Hyperion Press, 2003).

After discovering that she wasn't designed to live in a cubicle from nine to five, Margaret spent the year after her college graduation traveling, working part-time jobs, and wondering, *What the heck am I going to do with my life?* She finally decided that if she could do anything, she really wanted to write. So she sent query letters to a half-dozen Christian publications. Six years and some six hundred magazine articles later, she says she has found her niche.

Margaret has written *Simple Acts of Faith: Heartwarming Stories of One Life Touching Another,* and *God Whispers: Learning to Hear His Voice.* She also coauthored *Enjoying God: Embracing Intimacy with the Heavenly Father; I Am Relevant;* and *Cheap Ways to . . . (a Money Saving Guide).*

In 2003, Margaret finally said "I do" to a 6'8" Norwegian romantic who swept her off her feet. The couple currently reside in Sitka, Alaska, where Margaret has learned to kill Dungeness crabs with her bare hands and chase the northern lights. She enjoys hiking, kayaking, and, of course, salmon fishing. Despite excessive peer pressure and verbal taunting, she so far has managed to avoid the annual polar dip into the icy coastal waters. The couple hope to adopt a non-yippy, small dog very soon.

Margaret is passionate about writing, and she shares words of encouragement with other writers through an on-line writers' group called "The Fellowship," which sends out quarterly e-newsletters. To learn more about her work or receive *The Fellowship Newsletter,* visit Margaret on-line at www.margaretfeinberg.com.

To contact Margaret Feinberg on-line, visit her website at www.margaretfeinberg.com or e-mail her at mafeinberg@juno.com.

Printed in the United States
143834LV00001B/5/P